AF757416

Uzbekistan

TRANSITION TO AUTHORITARIANISM ON THE SILK ROAD

Neil J. Melvin

Routledge
Taylor & Francis Group
New York London

Copyright© 2000 OPA (Overseas Publishers Association) N.V. Published by license under the Harwood Academic Publishers imprint, part of The Gordon and Breach Publishing Group.

All rights reserved.

No part of this book may be reproduced or utilized in any form or by any means, electronic or mechanical, including photocopying and recording, or by any information storage or retrieval system, without permission in writing from the publisher. Printed in Singapore.

Amsteldijk 166
1st Floor
1079 LH Amsterdam
The Netherlands

British Library Cataloguing in Publication Data

A catalogue record for this book is available from the British Library.

ISBN: 9789058230294(hardcover)
ISBN; 9789058230300 (paperback)
ISSN: 978-9-0582-3029-4

Uzbekistan

Postcommunist States and Nations

Books in the series

Belarus: A denationalized nation
David R. Marples

Armenia: At the crossroads
Joseph R. Masih and Robert O. Krikorian

Poland: The conquest of history
George Sanford

Kyrgyzstan: Central Asia's island of democracy?
John Anderson

Ukraine: Movement without change, change without movement
Marta Dyczok

The Czech Republic: A nation of velvet
Rick Fawn

Uzbekistan: Transition to authoritarianism on the silk road
Neil J. Melvin

Romania: The unfinished revolution
Steven D. Roper

This book is part of a series. The publisher will accept continuation orders which may be cancelled at any time and which provide for automatic billing and shipping of each title in the series upon publication. Please write for details.

TABLE OF CONTENTS

CHRONOLOGY

7th century	Arab conquest and conversion to Islam within the ancient provinces of Sogdia and Bactria, particularly the cities of Samarkand and Bukhara.
13th century	Mongol conquest of the region.
1313–41	Rule of Uzbeg, after whom the Uzbek tribes were named.
1370–1405	Reign of Timur (Tamerlane), who established an empire centred upon Samarkand.
16th century	Uzbek tribes settle in core areas of Transoxiana, establishing dominance over the region, particularly Kokand, Samarkand, Bukhara and Khiva.
1867	Area of Karakalpakstan seized by Russian Empire.
1868	Emirate of Bukhara and Khanate of Kokand fall to the Russians and become protectorates.
1873	Khanate of Khiva becomes a protectorate of the Russian Empire.
1876	Abolition of the Khanate of Kokand.
30 April 1918	The Turkestan Autonomous Soviet Socialist Republic is formed including much of the territories of contemporary Uzbekistan.
September 1919	Soviet forces establish control over much of the region.
February 1920	Khiva falls to the Red Army and Khorezm People's Socialist Republic is founded.
September 1920	Emir of Bukhara flees in the face of the Red Army's advance. Declaration of Soviet Republic of Bukhara.
December 1922	Bukhara and Khorezm become founding units of the Soviet Union.
27 October 1924	The Uzbek Soviet Socialist Republic (UzSSR) is established.
1929	The Tajik ASSR, previously part of the UzSSR, becomes a full Union Republic of the USSR. The Khojand region of the UzSSR is also incorporated into the Tajik SSR.
1936	Karakalpakstan, formerly part of Kazakhstan, passes to the UzSSR.
1940	A Cyrillic script is imposed upon the Uzbek Latin script established in the late 1920s.
1943	The Muslim Board of Central Asia is founded in Tashkent, later a number of religious colleges and mosques are opened in Uzbekistan.
1959	Sharaf Rashidov becomes leader of the UzSSR.
1983	Death of Rashidov and exposure of a widespread fraud based upon the cotton crop of Uzbekistan.
1988	A group of Uzbek intellectuals founds *Birlik*.
June 1989	Ethnic rioting in the Fergana Valley between Uzbeks and Meskhetian Turk community. Islam Karimov becomes First Secretary of the Uzbek Communist Party.
October 1989	Uzbek becomes the state language.
24 March 1990	Islam Karimov is elected to the position of executive President.
20 June 1990	Uzbek declaration of sovereignty.
31 August 1991	The Supreme Soviet votes to declare the UzSSR independent and the next day the country becomes the Republic of Uzbekistan.

29 December 1991	Karimov is re-elected as President and on the same day 98.2% of voters support independence in a referendum.
November 1993	Uzbekistan introduces its own currency and leaves the Russian ruble zone.
January 1994	Uzbekistan signs an agreement with Kazakhstan and Kyrgyzstan to form an economic union.
Autumn 1995	First of several poor cotton harvests that leads to re-orientation of Uzbekistani economic policy.
January 1998	Uzbekistani authorities launch campaign against 'radical Islam'.
August 1998	Taliban forces in Afghanistan seize the territories in the north of the country previously controlled by Tashkent's ally.
January 1999	Bomb blasts in Tashkent prompt extensive crackdown against Islamic and opposition groups.

PREFACE

With the demise of the Soviet state at the end of 1991, Central Asia has emerged from a hundred years of relative obscurity. From being something of a backwater within the Soviet Union, within a few years Central Asia has been transformed into a region at the heart of the rapidly changing political, economic and social landscape of Eurasia. Uzbekistan lies at the core of Central Asia itself, a country bordering all of the other states of the region. Uzbekistan is the most populous country within Central Asia and is potentially the most powerful of the area's states. With the region's largest armed forces and strong ethnic and historic ties to territories in all the neighbouring states, Uzbekistan functions as the lynchpin to the whole Central Asian region.

The current volume is intended to serve as a broad introduction to Uzbekistan for those who have little experience of Central Asia but wish to learn more about the critical events and processes that have affected the territories and peoples of contemporary Uzbekistan. The book is divided into four chapters, each of which outlines a principal theme: history, politics, economics, and foreign relations. A short section at the conclusion of the volume entitled 'Further Reading' directs the reader to a selection of materials that offer a more in-depth treatment of the themes explored in the current study.

Chapter One examines the history and culture of Uzbekistan. Although Uzbekistan is a relatively new state, created as an administrative unit by Soviet planners in the early part of this century and achieving independence in 1991, the territories of contemporary Uzbekistan have played host to a rich past. Historically, the lands of modern Uzbekistan have been the home for a variety of important civilisations and empires. Powerful cities grew up across the region, fed by the trade of the Silk Road, the rich agricultural lands and the ability of the region's rulers to establish viable political and economic systems to harness the region's resources. The population of the area embraced Islam and in certain periods the region became a centre for advanced learning and culture.

Through the centuries, migrations, conquest and trade brought the population of the region into contact with a wide variety of peoples from Europe and Asia. The legacy of this historic mixing of peoples was the development of complex societies, built around a myriad of languages, communities and traditions. In the sixteenth century, Uzbek tribal groupings began to move into the region and soon emerged as powerful ruling clans across the region. In the nineteenth century, Russian colonisation of the kingdoms of Central Asia led to important changes in the geopolitical situation of the region, although much of the social and political structure of the area remained intact. In the 1920s, the establishment of Soviet control over the core territories of Central Asia led, however, to a fundamental transformation in the region.

Soon after seizing control of the area, Soviet planners undertook a series of policy initiatives that would reshape the region in many basic ways. The central element of the Soviet project in the region was the creation of the Uzbek Soviet Socialist Republic in 1924, the forerunner of the contemporary Uzbekistani state. Under Soviet tutelage, Uzbekistan and the Uzbek nation were forged as a single entity, linked to each other through language, a common history and, increasingly, a single economic and political infrastructure. In the final decades of the Soviet era, the Uzbek leadership was able to establish considerable autonomy from Moscow in the everyday running of the republic. More than any other factor, it was the changes introduced into Uzbekistan during the Soviet years that have shaped developments following independence.

Chapter Two of the volume is devoted to an examination of contemporary politics. The demise of Soviet control in Central Asia led to important changes in the political order in Uzbekistan. Critically, the role of the Communist Party has been supplanted by the emergence of an authoritarian executive system based around the person of the president, Islam Karimov. The ruthless suppression not simply of opposition forces but of all independent organisations and voices in Uzbekistan has provided the basis for a powerful centralised state to emerge based upon the unchecked use of coercion.

A leading figure in the Uzbek Communist Part before independence, President Karimov subsequently embraced nationalism as the justification for his rule. Consolidating an independent Uzbekistan and establishing stability within the borders of the state are the twin pillars of the new official orthodoxy. Uzbekistan, however, is home to a variety of peoples and cultures, and official nationalism has frequently appeared to threaten the position of the non-Uzbek residents of the country. Despite fears amongst the Uzbekistani elite about a political threat from democratic and human rights groups or the possibility of unrest amongst minorities, it is radical Islam that has emerged as potentially the most serious challenge to the post-independence order.

Since the late 1980s, Islam has become the single most difficult issue for the Karimov government. Islam is a thread that runs throughout most of Uzbekistani society and this has made the destruction of 'unofficial' religious groups problematic. Recognising the importance and power of Islam, the Uzbekistani government quickly embraced a 'moderate' form of religion in the early 1990s. Subsequently, however, the Karimov regime has had to engage in a delicate balancing act to prevent the emergence of more radical, or at least anti-government, forms of belief and religious organisation. The destruction of secular forms of opposition and the fusion of Islam with much of Uzbekistani society suggests, however, that Islam is likely to remain a problem for the current leadership and a potential block to the regime's aim of complete supremacy within the country. Critical to the ability of Karimov and his government to retain control will be its success in establishing a more prosperous society.

In Chapter Three of the book, the development and future prospects of the Uzbekistani economy are examined. The Soviet economic legacy in Uzbekistan is a mixed one. On the one hand, during the Soviet years Uzbekistan acquired elements of an advanced scientific and communications infrastructure, while on the other hand, the republican economy was developed primarily as the supplier of agricultural materials, and particularly for the production of cotton. The economic inheritance from the Soviet period has heavily constrained the ability of the Uzbekistani authorities to pursue economic development. The Karimov regime has, however, also failed to launch the range of reforms necessary to break free from the dependence on agricultural production previously established by Moscow's planners.

In the first years of independent existence, Uzbekistan seemed to be making important progress, particularly in relation to the economies of other former Soviet republics. The Uzbekistani authorities even seemed prepared to contemplate some limited forms of liberalisation in the economy. The poor harvests and low prices for cotton in the mid-1990s, however, exposed the fragile commitment to change in the country and set Uzbekistan on a path of autarkic economic management. Since 1995, the Uzbekistani economy has struggled to make any serious progress and instead has become increasingly harnessed to the overriding goal of establishing political stability in the country.

The failure to undertake the reforms necessary for the transformation of the Uzbekistani economy has stemmed from the ways in which Karimov's regime has developed. The emergence of a powerful authoritarian system has relied to a significant degree upon the elite's ability to manipulate the economy to its own advantage through corruption, advantageous government contracts and privileged access to financial and other resources. In order to construct this system, the state has not simply retained control of the Uzbekistani economy but has extended its reach into new types of business activities. While the Karimov political economy has provided the basis for the consolidation of an elite and its interests, a range of social pressures building up in Uzbekistan raise questions about the sustainability of this system. Rapid demographic growth, rising unemployment and increased competition for resources point to a future in which political unrest is likely to intensify around economic concerns.

Chapter Four of the volume is concerned with the external policy of Uzbekistan since the collapse of the Soviet system. Although the territory at the core of Central Asia has historically been a site of contest between competing kingdoms and empires, the engagement of Uzbekistan with the international system is a fundamentally new development. Since 1991 the Uzbekistani government has sought to build a set of relationships to the outside world that could help consolidate independence and the position of the Karimov regime. The primary driving force of external relations has been a search for links that can accelerate economic development in Uzbekistan. Reflecting this goal, Western industrial nations became the subject for the initial thrust of foreign policy. Building a relationship with the West was also perceived as the main means to establish political and security ties that would help consolidate the independent status of Uzbekistan.

Despite the goal of forging links to the West, particularly the United States, Tashkent has had to develop a variety of other relationships in response to a range of local and inter-regional issues. While the economic imperative remains the central thread of Uzbekistani external policy, security concerns have required a reorientation in some aspects of Uzbekistan's foreign relations. Significantly, the original strategy of promoting Uzbekistan as a country with little interest in close relations with the other former Soviet states has been supplanted by an increased stress upon co-operation, particularly in response to the rise of the Taliban in Afghanistan. Relations with other Central Asian states have grown more significant and the Russian Federation has re-emerged as an important security partner for Tashkent.

Since independence, Uzbekistan has succeeded in establishing a complex set of relationships to other states and also to a variety of interstate organisations. In many respects, the continual maneuvering by Tashkent has been successful in achieving many of its aims, however, the Uzbekistani leadership has yet to face a major international crisis. Moreover, in recent years Karimov's strategy towards Tajikistan and Afghanistan has collapsed prompting a redirection of external policy. The significant shift in Uzbekistan's external policies suggests that as the country faces increased external challenges in the future, Tashkent may struggle to retain a strong independent position.

In writing this book I have incurred a number of debts. Firstly I would like to thank those in Uzbekistan and Central Asia who have offered me help in collecting material for this volume and who have shaped my understanding of developments in the region in general and Uzbekistan in particular. For reasons of safety, individuals cannot be mentioned. I would also like to thank an anonymous reviewer who suggested many important revisions to an earlier version. Finally, I would like to dedicate this work to E.

Map of Uzbekistan

Chapter 1

HISTORY AND CULTURE

INTRODUCTION

In the twentieth century, Uzbekistan has emerged as home to the most powerful and populous political community in Central Asia. The appearance of Uzbekistan on the world stage is, however, a comparatively new phenomenon. Moreover, the Uzbek community itself is of relatively recent origin. Edward Allworth argues that the roots of Uzbek history can be traced to the fourteenth century. He thereby challenges the thesis popular among Soviet and Uzbek historians that the beginnings of Uzbek society and politics stretch back to the ancient civilisations of Central Asia, such as Achemedia, Bactria, Sogdia and Tokaria, and the rule of Alexander of Macedonia.[1]

Other scholars have suggested that the label 'Uzbek' only acquired a political and socio-cultural significance in the twentieth century as a result of Soviet policies of nation-founding. Indeed, Uzbek nationhood may be considered one of the most successful Soviet-era inventions. While incomplete at the time of independence, the Soviet nation-building project in the Uzbek Soviet Socialist Republic nevertheless laid the basis for the emergence of the current nationalism in the area.

Establishing the relationship between past and present in Uzbekistan is a contentious project but, at the same time, an intrinsic part of the process whereby the modern political community is constituted. Contemporary Uzbekistan has clearly been shaped by political, cultural and economic history and it would be foolish to suggest that the identities of the current populations of Uzbekistan have not been influenced by the past. The key issue is the way in which the link between past and present is formulated and the way in which elements of the past that are abstracted to establish a dominant, official historical narrative, that all too frequently excludes the past of minorities.

Contemporary accounts of history in Uzbekistan reflect the project to merge real and imagined events, persons and places in a coherent and largely seamless vision of the past. Within this project, interpretations of the pre-colonial, Russian imperial and Soviet periods are being used to legitimate and discredit forms of political power and organisation. The past has become the prism through which contemporary political struggle is refracted.

While the visible elements of the contemporary struggle for the past are debates about important figures in history, the role and nature of core cultures and languages, and the military, scientific and political character of past regimes, the central purpose of these debates is less obvious. Fundamental understandings about the nature, boundaries and origins of the contemporary political community are being forged. At the centre of this debate is a struggle to define the nature of the Uzbek nation and its relationship to the past. Critically, it is important to be clear that the terms Uzbekistan, the Uzbek community and the territory of Uzbekistan have only been established as an interrelated, indeed inseparable, set of ideas in recent history.

Examination of the history of the territories of contemporary Uzbekistan is thus clearly an important subject because it tells us much about contemporary society. More than this though, the past of the Transoxiana region is worthy of consideration for the fascinating and rich nature of history of the area. For the sake of simplicity, the history of the region can be divided into three main periods: early history; the Russian colonial era; and the Soviet period.

EARLY HISTORY

The territories of the Republic of Uzbekistan have been populated for thousands of years and have served as the centre for a variety of civilisations, cultures and peoples. The earliest recorded inhabitants of the region were Persian-speaking peoples who inhabited the valleys of the Syr Darya (Jaxartes) and Amu Darya (Oxus) rivers. The plains to the north of the Syr Darya were largely populated by Scythians, as well as Persian-speakers, and groups of nomads.

The area between the two great rivers was identified by Persian and Arabic historians as the Transoxiana region. By the sixth century BC, Transoxiana was the location for two kingdoms. The Persian monarch Cyrus the Great founded the city of Cyropolis on the banks of the Jaxartes, while the Bactrian kingdom, centred in what is today Afghanistan, controlled the territories along much of the Oxus.

In the fourth century BC Alexander the Great passed through Central Asia on the way to conquer India. The Central Asia of this era consisted largely of city states. The Sogdian kingdom at this time was centred upon the city of Samarkand. Khorezm, situated in the west of today's Uzbekistan, was already an independent region. Popular beliefs hold that Alexander was the founder of Samarkand, although most historians discount this version of the past. In fact, many Central

Asian cities were renamed in honour of Alexander, and he remains a folk hero in the region to this day.

Following the death of Alexander, Greek influence in Central Asia declined, and the region fell under the influence of the Parthian empire. With the rise of the Samanid dynasty in Persia, the influence of Baghdad was replaced by Persian influence. Bukhara emerged as a major trading region and eventually became the capital of the Samanid dynasty.

During this period, the first Turkic invasions of Central Asia from the north occurred. Often destructive, the Turkic invaders left little of lasting significance from their early forays. The arrival of Turkic invaders nevertheless indicated the future political trajectory of Central Asia; although it was not to be until the thirteenth century that the Turkic presence in Central Asia became permanent.

Between the time of the first invasions and the conquest of Central Asia by Turkic tribes, several important external forces were to influence the development of the region in important ways. Arab armies came to Central Asia following the death of Muhammad in 632. In the century following his death, the Arab empire grew to stretch from North Africa and Spain in the west to Asia Minor and Persia in the east. The Arabs arrived in Central Asia in the middle of the seventh century, reaching Merv in 651. But the Arab advance faced opposition and was not able to penetrate deep into the region until later decades. Over the next century, Arab influence grew incrementally, eventually coming to encompass all the major settled regions of Central Asia.

The Arab arrival brought important change in the form of science, new cultural forms and, in particular, Islam. Direct rule by the Arabs was relatively short, but their real importance lay with the ideas and cultural patterns left behind. Arabic became the language of science and commerce in the region for the next three hundred years, while the Arabic script persisted until the Soviet era. Islam emerged as the dominant and almost exclusive religion of the region, displacing other forms of belief to the margins of Central Asian society.

During the Dark Ages in Europe, scholarship and knowledge prospered in Central Asia. The rich legacy of Arabic learning was particularly important in the oases cities of Khorezm and Bukhara. During this period, a variety of notable scholars and thinkers were active, including Al Khwarezm, Abu Rai Raihan Al Biruni, and Abu Ali Ibn Sina.

By the turn of the millennium, Samanid rule had collapsed and such power and authority as existed passed into the hands of the Turkic invaders who swept through the region at this time. In the thirteenth century, the Mongol chieftain, Chingis Khan, descended upon Transoxiana, attacking the main oasis settlements. He captured the great cities of Bukhara and Samarkand in about 1225 and subsequently Central Asia fell under the control of various Mongol tribal chieftains. In 1227, the Mongol leader died leaving a vast empire for his descendants, who divided up the newly conquered territories.

Under the rule of Chingis Khan and his heirs, much of Eurasia was united for the first time. The rule of the Mongols was, however, far from benign. Many of the great cities of Central Asia were destroyed, as was much of the irrigation system that lay at the heart of settled life in the region. The common political space established by Mongol rule nevertheless laid the basis for the emergence of a vibrant pattern of commerce in the two succeeding centuries. Under Mongol rule, the great trade routes of the Silk Road began to flourish.

The rule of Chingis Khan and his descendants also left a continuing cultural legacy in the form of the Turkic languages. Prior to the thirteenth century invasions, Turkic languages were already widely used in Central Asia, however, with Mongol conquest the importance of these languages was to change significantly. While the Mongol leaders spoke a common language, the waves of settlers that moved to Central Asia accompanying Mongol domination brought a variety of other Turkic languages to the region.

The destruction of the main Arabic and Persian centres of learning also helped Turkic languages to become prominent in the region. Persian and Arabic nonetheless continued to be important in the fields of science and learning. While the Turkic dynasties became ascendant, the traditions of Islam continued to prosper.

In the centuries following Mongol conquest important changes occurred in the political, economic and cultural make-up of the Transoxiana region and the territories bordering the core area of Central Asia. During this period, Turkic and Islamic traditions underwent a process of mutual assimilation. At the same time, Turkic-based languages became more important, displacing the previous dominance of Persian and Arabic in key areas. By the fifteenth century, the Mongol language of the ruling elite had been replaced by other Turkic languages.

One of the most important descendants of Chingis Khan was Timur the Lame (known as Tamerlane in Europe, 1336–1405). In about 1350, Timur moved his rule from the city of Kish to Samarkand, which became the centre for one of the last great empires focused upon Central Asia. Timur built a powerful military force and, following Chingis Khan before him, he set out to conquer the then known world. He invaded Persia, the Siberian plains and also entered Anatolia, capturing Ankara in 1402. But Timur was the last of the leaders who succeeded in unifying Central Asia.

Following Timur's death, subsequent leaders were unable to reunite Central Asia as a single 'Turkestan'. Timur's grandson, Ulugh-bek (1394–1449) was a ruler and leading scientist. He failed, however, to follow the expansionist policies of his grandfather. Zahiriddin Babur (1483–1530), a Timurid leader, had his imperial ambitions frustrated by the tribal fragmentation within Central Asia, and turned his energies to the south. Babur marched through Afghanistan and on to India where he founded the Mughal empire.

Despite Timur's efforts to build a powerful empire in Central Asia, by the fourteen century Mongol influence was in decline and Central Asia became a patchwork of small principalities. The political organisation of the region was characterised by continually shifting alliances, and the growth and contraction of kingdoms. The decline of the Mongol dynasty and the fragmentation of territories once united under Mongol rule was accompanied by the emergence of the Uzbek tribal confederation as a powerful force, particularly in the settled areas of Transoxiana.

Early in the sixteenth century, Central Asia came under the control of the Uzbek tribes moving from the steppe regions of the north and led by Muhammad Shaibani Khan. The emergence of the Uzbeks as an important force in Central Asia was of particular importance. The Shaibanid invasion accelerated the disintegration and fragmentation of the political arrangements of the Mongol era. Reflecting the significance of this development, the Soviet authorities gave special support for work on the origins of the Uzbeks in Central Asia and Uzbek ethnogenesis in this period. Establishing the ethnic origins of the Uzbeks was central to the Soviet project of developing a socialist Uzbek nation. Despite the work of Soviet scholars, the nature and significance of the emergence of the Uzbeks continues to be contentious and contested.

Edward Allworth notes the development of the Uzbek tribal confederation in the areas of Khorezm in the west of Uzbekistan and in the area to the north of the Aral Sea in the fifteenth century. He stresses, however, that the consolidation of the Uzbeks was built upon the coming together of Turkic tribes, with the term Uzbek having a tribal rather than ethnic meaning. '... the Uzbek group, like many ethnic entities in the modern world, cannot reach into a distant past to anchor itself to an earlier counterpart. Both discontinuity with the past and insecure linkage between name and group complicate present Uzbek existence as well as the process of understanding the problem. The geographical distribution of people added to this complexity.'[2]

The consolidation of the Uzbek tribal confederation was accompanied by a migration to the south, into the core regions of Central Asia. Members of the confederation began to take control of the settled areas of Transoxiana from the fifteenth century and to mix with the peoples already in the region. Despite the migration of the Uzbek tribes, the groups within the confederation were widely dispersed and ethnically indistinct. Uzbek power was finally consolidated at the beginning of the sixteenth century when Muhammed Shaibani seized control of the last independent kingdoms in the region. Thereafter, the term Uzbek was associated with the several dynasties descended from Shaibani that ruled the region.

As the Uzbeks took control of Transoxiana, their previously nomadic lifestyle began to give way to a sedentary existence. Many Uzbeks settled in the cities and towns of the region and began to assimilate with the previous inhabitants of the region, including other Turkic peoples and Persian-speakers. While retaining their tribal identification, the sedentary Uzbeks simultaneously identified themselves with other settled peoples under the general label of *Sart*.

The essential division that emerged in Central Asian society in this period was between *Sarts* and nomads. These were socio-economic categories, although categories that were also marked by important cultural distinctions based upon language and religion. Elite level bilingualism became an important part of the region's identity with the political life of the court conducted predominantly in a Turkic language (Chagatai), while high culture was largely the province of Persian. Contemporary historians are divided about the nature of cultural divisions in this period, with many Uzbek interpretations identifying the noted writer of this period, Alisher Navoi (1441–1501), as the father of Uzbek literature. There were also important minority communities in the region, notably Central Asian Jews.

From the seventeenth century, the previously united Uzbek khanate began to fragment and was replaced by smaller, highly autonomous kingdoms or khanates. Initially, the two most powerful khanates were Bukhara and Khiva. From the eighteenth century, however, the Khanate of Kokand, centred on Fergana, began to rival the other two. The near constant state of conflict between these states assisted Russian conquest of the region.

On the eve of Russian conquest, the power of Central Asia's kingdoms relative to that of their neighbours had declined significantly from previous centuries. By the seventeenth century the fragmentation of political power in the central region of Central Asia had produced three khanates, disunited and lacking well-defined borders, each led by a powerful khan: Kokand in the Fergana Valley; Bukhara in the Zerafshan Valley; and Khiva in the west on the Amu River. The Bukharan ruler continued the Persian influence of earlier centuries, maintaining the title of emir.

In the eighteenth and nineteenth century, the dominant form of society was feudal slave owning and the economy was built around agriculture and handicrafts. A strong set of cultural traditions existed around the idea of deference and respect for elders and the more powerful. Society was structured around patriarchal forms with strict hierarchies for male and female groups. Islam continued to be an important factor in society and Islamic leaders also operated in an uneasy relationship with the dynastic political leaders. While trade remained important, from the sixteenth century the Silk Road entered a period of decline with the development of global sea travel.

RUSSIAN CONQUEST

The relative decline of Central Asia from the sixteenth century was matched by the steady expansion of Russian imperial power. The competition between external empires and the stagnating kingdoms of Central Asia reached its climax in the latter half of the nineteenth century. In this period, Central Asia became the location for a complex series of struggles as imperial powers, native rulers, conservatives, and modernisers fought for control over the region.[3]

In the fifteenth century under the leadership of Ivan III (Ivan the Great), Russia began to unify following two centuries of domination by the Mongols. The expansion of the Russian empire from the core territories on the European plains began to gather pace in the sixteenth century. The troops of Ivan IV (Ivan the Terrible) captured the Tatar city of Kazan in 1552. Soon after this, the Turkic populations of the Volga region were incorporated into the Russian empire.

In the seventeenth century the Russian empire spread deep into Siberia. Over the next two centuries, the Russian empire pushed eastward and southwards across the steppe regions of Central Asia reaching the northern edge of the Kazakh Steppe by the 1820s. Gradually the local tribes were absorbed into the Russian colonial system. As the borders of the Russian empire approached the periphery of Central Asia, various attempts were made to conquer the core areas of Central Asia. It proved, however, to be the latter half of the nineteenth century before Russian conquest of the Transoxiana region was effected.

By the mid-nineteenth century, the population of the Bukharan Emirate was about two and a half million. Russian accounts identify about half of the population as Uzbeks, one third Tajiks, and one tenth Turkmen, however, the ambiguous nature of ethnic identification in this period make establishing definitive numbers problematic. The lands of the Khan of Khiva were located south of the Aral Sea focused upon the oasis of Khiva. The Khivan Khanate had a population of three-quarters of a million, consisting of a mixture of Karakalpaks, Turkmen, Kazakhs and Uzbeks. Finally, Kokand controlled large territories, between the Syr Daria and Muslim China, with its centre located in the Fergana Valley and the Tashkent oasis. The population was about three million, mostly Uzbeks, Kazakhs and Kyrgyz. Various groups of nomadic populations were found on the periphery of these mini-empires.

Initially, Russian attempts to conquer the kingdoms at the heart of Central Asia were unsuccessful. In 1719, a disastrous expedition to capture Khiva was launched under Prince A. Bekovich-Cherkasskii. In 1839, a second expedition was sent to Khiva, this time led by General Perovskii, but it also failed. From the mid-nineteenth century, however, several factors combined to help the Russian advance. Of central importance to Russian victory was the development of a communications infrastructure within the imperial territories that provided a means to move men and materiel to the frontiers.

Russian troops conquered important parts of Kokand in the key Fergana Valley as early as 1853, but Central Asia did not become the central focus for Russian imperial expansion until defeat in the Crimean War (1854–56). Following the war, Anglo-Russian competition became more intense as Russia sought to counter British advances through India. As a result, the Russian drive to subordinate the heart of Central Asia became that much more urgent. In what became know as the 'Great Game', Russia and Britain vied for control of Central Asia.

The new Russian advance into the heart of Central Asia began in 1860 with a movement south along the Syr Darya river toward the Kyrgyz mountains. The town of Pishpek was seized in 1860 and Turkestan, Aulie-Ata and Chimkent in 1864, thus linking eastern and western lines of forts and enclosing the Kazakh Steppe. Within days, the conqueror of Chimkent, General M. G. Cherniaev, launched an abortive assault upon Tashkent, the economic centre of the Kokand khanate.

In conquering Central Asia, Russia was assisted by the conflict between the three kingdoms of Bukhara, Khiva and Kokand. Rivalry between these kingdoms ensured that they failed to co-operate effectively to resist Russian advances. In June 1865, Cherniaev successfully took Tashkent. Three years later he seized the town of Samarkand, turning the Emirate of Bukhara into a Russian protectorate (1868). At the same time, a treaty was concluded with the rump of the Kokand khanate formalising its dependence on Russia. By 1873, Khiva had met a similar fate and in 1876 Russia abolished the khanate of Kokand and its territory was absorbed into the Russian Empire.

Having taken control of the Central Asian kingdoms, Russia turned its attention to the Turkmen tribes. Following a bloody battle fought in January 1881 at the fortress of Geok-tepe, which ended with the massacre of the native population, the last territories of Central Asia fell under Russian control. The subordination of the Turkmen tribes marked the end of serious resistance to Russian colonial rule in the region, leaving rebellion as the only form of opposition for the Central Asian populations in the decades ahead. Both Britain and Russia brought the struggle to control Central Asia to an end with an agreement in 1885 to demarcate the external borders of the region.

With the military conquest of Central Asia complete, the Russian conquerors sought to consolidate their rule in the region and to integrate the new territories into the empire. At first, the Russian government did not demand complete control of the protectorates, letting the local leaders rule in a tributary relationship to St. Petersburg. The khanates retained their native rulers, and a degree of political autonomy. The territory of the Kokand khanate, which had put up the most resistance to Russian invasion and controlled the best agricultural land, was placed directly under the control of the governor-general as early as 1876.

The integration of the Kazakh lands and Turkestan into the Russian empire was in large part an *ad hoc* process initially undertaken by the military. The Kazakh Steppe was divided into six regions, two controlled by the authorities in the Russian town of Orenburg, two by the city of Omsk and two regions (Syr Darya and Semirechie) by the Turkestan Governor-Generalship, which had been established in 1867 and was based in Tashkent. The first governor-general was General K. P. von Kaufman (1867–81). General von Kaufman had been operating from Orenburg previously, and now he moved his headquarters to Tashkent. It became the seat of the Governor-Generalship and later grew to become the most important city in Central Asia.

In 1867 a decree was issued uniting the former kingdoms under Russian administration as the Province (*guberniia*) of Turkestan. The first formal tsarist administrative structures were established shortly after the decree of 1867. The decree specified a two-tiered administrative arrangement recognising a distinction between the cultural lives of the native population and the colonising Russians.

Tsarist policy was designed to ensure continued domination while interfering as little as possible with native religion, customs and lifestyles. At the local level, administration was largely left in the hands of the native administrators, with customary courts retaining jurisdiction over all the most serious cases. In the early years of the Russian colonial regime in Central Asia, General von Kaufman resisted efforts to bring Orthodox missionaries to the region to challenge Islam. After von Kaufman's resignation in 1881, a more liberal policy was rejected. Religious schools began to merge with Russian literacy schools and some religious property (*waqf*) designed for the upkeep of schools was seized. From the 1880s, the pilgrimage to Mecca became more difficult. But the main drive for education reform came not from the Russian authorities but from the 'new method' schools created by the pan-Turkic inspired Jadid movement.

The Turkestan region was divided into a number of districts each presided over by a military governor subordinate to the governor-general in Tashkent. The interest of the military leaders was, however, more often in territorial expansion or personal gain than in civilian administration. Resistance to the local Russian rulers, who were frequently involved in running fiefdoms, led to popular revolts in 1889.

The riots produced a government report that criticised the Russian policy of non-interference in the cultural affairs for abetting the growth of pan-Islamic propaganda.

Although the general thrust of the Russian colonial regime was toward weak direct engagement with Central Asia society, there were three areas where Russian involvement did expand greatly following conquest of the region: cotton production, the settlement of Russians and other Slavs, and the growth of Russian-Central Asian trade. These changes produced important shifts in the social and political structures of the region and brought the population of Central Asia into contact with new political ideas and identities.

Under Russian rule, cotton production grew, displacing many other forms of agricultural produce. One of the first tasks undertaken by the Russian colonial authorities in Central Asia was the reconstruction and extension of the region's irrigation system. The renewed irrigation network provided the basis for a growth in cotton production. In the last two decades of the nineteenth century cotton output increased more than eight times. At the same time, food imports to the region began to rise as cotton output displaced food production, notably in the Fergana Valley.

With Russian domination came an influx of settlers from the core regions of the empire, notably peasants from European Russia. The majority of the migrants moved onto the steppe regions of the north (present day Kazakhstan), reflecting the then popular perception that these lands were unoccupied. While Turkestan was far less affected by Russian settlement that the nomadic areas to the north, important European populations developed in the main cities of the region, notably Tashkent, the administrative centre of Russian rule.

A particularly important aspect of colonial consolidation in Central Asia was the economic integration of the region into the rest of the empire. The development of a transport infrastructure to move troops and materiel to the edge of Central Asia had been a crucial element in Russia's ability to conquer Central Asia at the end of the nineteenth century. Following conquest, the economic integration of the region was facilitated by the extension of the railways into Central Asia. A railway line was extended to Samarkand from the Caspian Sea and then to Tashkent. By 1906, the Orenburg-Tashkent line was complete.

With a transport infrastructure in place, Russian economic development of Central Asia began to accelerate. Russian investment was largely concentrated upon trade and the production of cotton, rather than industrial development. Although industries related to textile production did begin to develop in some of the important urban centres. The changing nature of economic activity in the region was accompanied my new political ideas, ideas that frequently placed the native population in opposition to the Russian colonial authorities.

During the early years of colonial rule in Central Asia, the Russian authorities faced little sustained opposition from the local population. However, in 1898 a rising in Andizhan shattered the relative calm of the region. Local religious and secular groups used peasant unrest in the area to challenge Russian control. Unlike the steppe regions of the north, where native discontent was usually focused on the rising numbers of Russian settlers, in the Turkestan region hostility was directed against local administrators, many of whom were not Russian.

The 1905 Revolution in Russia left Central Asia largely untouched. Revolutionary activity in the region was focused mostly amongst the Slavic settlers. Nevertheless, during these years, peasant unrest did increase, particularly as a result of disputes over land and water. The economic and technological changes introduced by the Russian colonial regime also had an important impact. The development of cotton production in the region and the increased links to the outside world as a result of the introduction of trains and telegraph communication fostered new debates and conflicts in Central Asia.

In the early part of the twentieth century the key debate to emerge in Central Asia was between the modernist movements, who argued for the incorporation of new ideas and some western values into Central Asian society, and the conservatives, who opposed many of these ideas. The Russian authorities were particularly concerned by the activities of reformist organisations amongst the Central Asians, notably the rise of pan-Turkic movements.

The most important of the pan-Turkic movements was the Jadids, who stressed education and literacy. In the early part of the twentieth century there was a considerable expansion of Jadid schools in Central Asia. In the years following the 1905 Revolution, more than 100 'new method' schools were opened in Turkestan. Often the pan-Turkic movement was fiercely opposed by native religious and secular elites who felt threatened by organisations expousing new ideas such as the 'Young Bukharans'.

While Central Asians had been only marginally involved in the 1905 Revolution, the consequences of this event produced an important shift in the political orientation of key sections of the Central Asian elites. Russia's constitutional experiment led to the election of Muslims from Turkestan to the second Duma. At the same time, the ferment of ideas around the 1905 Revolution helped produce the first nationalist movements in Central Asia, notably with the creation of *Alash Orda* in the northern steppe regions in December 1905.

The Russian authorities interpreted unrest in 1905 outside the core imperial territories as emanating from the communities most influenced by contact with the Russian empire. As a result, modernists were seen as the greatest threat to the Russian imperial regime in Central Asia. To counter the perceived threat of pan-Turkic organisations in the early years of the twentieth century, the previous Russian policy of non-interference was replaced with one in which the Russian imperial regime came to ally itself with the most conservative elements in Central Asia.

Russian conquest of the region also introduced important economic and cultural changes. Tashkent, previously a minor town, became the capital of Russian Turkestan and home to a sizeable Russian population. Russian language, technology and administration spread rapidly in the region. Significant changes in agriculture were introduced, notably improved irrigation for growing cotton.

In the early decades of the twentieth century a variety of less welcome changes were also under way in Central Asia, including the seizure of land, the destruction of nomadic lifestyles, and the creation of a landless peasantry. Most of these changes were, however, concentrated in the steppe regions, while the core regions of Central Asia remained relatively unaffected. Russian conquest did little to alter fundamentally the way of life for the peoples in these regions.

Some Tsarist policies did, however, cause particular hostility among the communities of the Transoxiana region. The imposition of taxes (notably war taxes) placed special economic burdens on the native population. Demands placed upon Central Asian in support of Russian efforts in World War One were especially unpopular, particularly the Mobilisation Decree of June 1916 calling for Central Asian men to be drafted for support activities. Hostility to this decree produced a widespread uprising, which in some parts of the Fergana Valley acquired a religious character. The revolt spread to the plains, where it became more bloody in character. The Central Asian uprising was only put down just prior to the onset of the Bolshevik Revolution.

REVOLUTION

The shock waves caused by the collapse of the imperial regime in 1917 spread quickly to the regions of Central Asia. Initially, the Provisional Government in St. Petersburg created a Turkestan Committee based upon the old Governor-Generalship, but in both Turkestan and the steppe towns local Soviets began to emerge. In Turkestan a situation of dual power developed, although by the autumn of 1917 Soviet power was advancing. After winning over the Tashkent garrison, the local Soviet formally seized power a week ahead of the actions by the Bolsheviks in Petrograd. The action in Tashkent, however, only signalled a prolonged period of uncertainty. In the following years, the region was subject to control by competing forces—the British, the Whites and the nationalist *Basmachi* movement—and it was not until September 1919 that Soviet control of Turkestan was re-established.

Following the October events, the young Soviet regime in Turkestan was almost immediately cut off from Soviet Russia by White forces, and remained so with a few interruptions until 1919, when a Bolshevik apparatus was consolidated in Turkestan. During the period of isolation from the Soviet regime in Russia, the power of the Tashkent Soviet stretched little further than the city limits. In particular, the authorities of Tashkent were too weak to control events in the former Russian protectorates of Khiva and Bukhara, where new political forces and movements appeared amongst the native population.

The October Revolution in Central Asia was initially a settlers affair and the creation of the Soviets tended to reflect the colonial population's interests. The number of communists in Tashkent was small, the first Party Conference, which took place in June 1918, had only 250 party members in the entire city. Faced with the challenge of the Whites, British forces to the south and increasing political activism among the native population, the Tashkent Soviet sought support amongst the settler population, particularly the Russian workers of the Tashkent Railroad Repair Shops and the troops of the local garrison. Even by the Third Congress of Soviets, there was no Muslim representation. As a result, in the years immediately following the Revolution, conflicts in Turkestan were heavily informed by struggles between settler and native interests, as opposed to the struggle of communism versus liberalism and monarchy, which informed the political struggles to the north.

At the same time, Muslims also became politically active but they faced problems organising in the face of ethnic, regional, and ideological differences. The key issue for the native population was a debate about the future relationship to Russia following the political changes of the Revolution. Both the Provisional Government and the Soviets were committed to maintaining the Russian control of the region. Demands for greater autonomy came from the various Muslim conferences held in Turkestan during 1917.

The Fourth Congress of Central Asian Muslims was held in Kokand in December 1917. A national council was elected and the Congress repeated earlier calls for autonomy from Russian control. The Congress was dominated by representatives from the cities of Bukhara and Khiva, but also contained important numbers of local Slavs. Following the declaration of autonomy, a position of dual power emerged in Turkestan. To counter the political power of the Congress of Muslims in February 1918 the forces of the Tashkent Soviet seized Kokand and massacred many of its inhabitants.

In 1918, tensions between Bolshevik leaders in Russia, the Tashkent Soviet and native leaders intensified. The Bolshevik regime in Russia initiated attempts to moderate the activities of the Tashkent Soviet. The aim of the Bolshevik authorities was to bring the Tashkent political forces under central control and to integrate the native Muslims into the Communist Party and the state administration.

The first stage on the path to establishing centralised control came on 30 April 1918 with the establishment of the Turkestan Autonomous Soviet Socialist Republic (TASSR). The TASSR was constituted within a territory that included Uzbekistan. Soon after this, the Soviet troops were forced to withdraw temporarily when confronted by the nationalist *Basmachi* movement supported by British and White forces. In September 1919, Soviet forces re-established control of much of present day territory of Uzbekistan. At the same time, a drive to recruit Muslims into the Communist Party was launched.

In late 1919 the arrival of the Soviet troops from the north, which followed the reestablishment of communications between Turkestan and Russia, moved the balance of power in Tashkent from the local authorities to the representatives from Moscow and the military command of the Red Army. The Bolshevik leadership sought to broaden the base of support in Turkestan beyond the settler population by drawing the native population into regional political arrangements. In November 1919, the Turkestan Commission was created to purge many of the Tashkent veterans from the local Soviet.

During the Civil War, the Bolsheviks had largely left the Khivan and Bukharan Protectorates alone, although providing support for the more radical elements within these regions. In February 1920 Khiva fell to the Red Army and on April 4 1920 it was transformed into the People's Republic of Khorezm. In September 1920 the Emir of Bukhara fled the city, and the territory of the Emirate was conquered by the Red Army. A Soviet People's Republic of Bukhara, also nominally independent, was declared in early 1921. Despite the transformation of these kingdoms and the flight of the Emir, the former Russian protectorates remained the source of a potential challenge to the new Bolshevik regime in Central Asia.

Once the period of isolation ended, the political situation began to change quickly in Central Asia. Muslim participation in the new regime increased and the idea of self-determination gained increasing currency among native intellectuals. Soviet domination appeared to be complete but a new threat, in the form of 'national communism' in Bukhara and Khiva, now arose and a Muslim nationalist revolt across the region appeared to threaten Bolshevik control. Of particular importance were the groups of nationalists know as the Young Bukharans and Young Khivans.

The *Basmachis* also posed a significant threat to the Bolshevik's hold over Central Asia. In response to the harsh policies of the Tashkent Soviet and the bloody crushing of the Kokand autonomy, small guerrilla forces emerged across Central Asia. Together, these groups constituted the *Basmachi* movement, which was particularly active in the Fergana Valley and in 1919 controlled much of the region. In 1921 the Turkish leader Enver Pasha joined the movement but was killed by Bolshevik forces in April 1922.

Faced by the growing challenge of the native nationalist movement, in 1921–22 the Bolsheviks made concessions in terms of the national and religious demands of the local population. Grain requisitioning was ended, and mosques and *waqf* property was returned. By 1922, the *Basmachi* movement had been defeated in the peripheral areas of Central Asia, and by 1922–23 the Bolsheviks had taken formal control of the region as a whole. So began a new phase, with the integration of Central Asia into a centralised Soviet political regime located in Russia.

At the heart of the new Bolshevik policy in Central Asia was a series of territorial reorganisations with the ostensible aim of giving the native nationalists some form of local autonomy. Lenin's notion of autonomy while limiting Muslim aspirations provided the basis for co-operation between the Bolshevik regime and the nationalist elite—this action effectively undermined support for the *Basmachis*. The Turkestan ASSR was formed in April 1921 and in December 1922 Bukhara and Khorezm were founding members of the USSR. Gradually, however, pressure was placed on Khorezm and Bukhara and in 1924 they were incorporated into the Soviet Union.

SOVIET UZBEKISTAN

The establishment of Bolshevik power in Central Asia was accompanied by an important set of policies that aimed to consolidate Soviet control and transform the communities of the region into a communist society. Soviet policies were focused upon restructuring the administrative structure of Central Asia, creating new identities in the form of national communities, drawing native personnel into Communist political structures and modernising society as a whole. Together, these policies were to lay the foundations for the emergence of contemporary Uzbekistan and the Uzbek nation.[4]

In the period 1924–25, the Bolsheviks initiated the first stage of a programme of national delimitation in Central Asia. Under this programme, pre-colonial and Tsarist administrative arrangements were replaced by new divisions. Officially, the new territorial units of Central Asia were based upon national communities, but more often the changes were intended to provide the administrative vehicles by which such communities could be brought into being. On 27 October 1924 the Uzbek Soviet Socialist Republic (UzSSR) was established by merging most of the territories of the three former khanates of Turkestan. The project to create the Uzbek Republic was promoted strongly by Faizulla Khojaev and other Young Bukharans who had formed an alliance with the Bolsheviks following the end of the Civil War.

In May 1925 the UzSSR became a constituent republic of the Union of Soviet Socialist Republics (USSR). At the time, the establishment of the UzSSR was seen by many in Central Asia as the reincarnation of a Greater Bukhara. By the end of 1925, this seemed to be the case, with the incorporation of the Fergana Valley into the UzSSR while the newly created administrative region of Tajikistan was given only a subordinate status within the new Republic. In Central Asia, only Turkmenistan was initially given the same status of the UzSSR, that of a union republic, while the lands of the Kazakh Steppe were only granted the rank of an autonomous area (ASSR) within the Russian Federation.

In subsequent changes to the boundaries of the UzSSR, the position of pre-eminence previously enjoyed by the republic was weakened. Tajikistan was granted the status of a full union republic in its own right in 1929. The Tajik SSR also gained parts of the Khojand (Leninabad) area of the Fergana Valley, much to the chagrin of the elites in the UzSSR. In 1936 the Karakalpak ASSR, the region to the south east of the Aral Sea, passed from Kazakhstan (previously part of the Russian Federation) to the Uzbek SSR.

Although the territorial delimitation of Central Asia was officially conducted on ethno-linguistic lines, the aim of these changes was to promote the emergence of ethnic and national identities, but heavily informed by a socialist consciousness. Soviet policy-makers intended the UzSSR to become the ethnic homeland for Uzbeks. In the census conducted in the region following the creation of the UzSSR, minority Turkic groups and many bi-lingual Tajiks were categorised together with the Uzbeks, thereby swelling the numbers of the titular population. Larger minorities such as Kazakhs, Kyrgyz and Tajiks, however, continued to enjoy a separate ethnic identity.

By 1924 Moscow had established *de jure* control over Turkestan but it still faced the task of remaking the region in the Bolshevik image. Much of the Soviet period was marked by a continuing drive to achieve the transformation of Central Asian society and to entrench the administrative changes of the 1920s. The territorial reorganisation that led to the creation of Uzbekistan within its present boundaries was accompanied by a set of policies designed to consolidate the new administrative system. The purpose of these policies was two fold: to tie the new republic firmly to the core of the Soviet system, and; to develop national and socialist identities within the administrative districts defined by the Soviet planners.

A critical task that faced the Soviet authorities was to integrate the native population into new political structures subordinated to the centre. Initially, the new policies were intended to placate the native elites and their nationalist aspirations. As Soviet power became stronger and Stalin moved to a position of pre-eminence, the early reforms were replaced by more radical policies that transformed Soviet Uzbekistan.

The Communist Party was the key vehicle to achieve this aim, but party organisations were weak in Uzbekistan. Following Soviet conquest of Central Asia, the recruitment of native communists therefore became a priority. Particularly important was the co-option of much of the former native nationalist elite such as the Young Bukharans. Problems in recruiting native personnel were accentuated by low levels of literacy and education that remained until the late 1930s.

In response to the need to raise native recruitment, the policy of *korenizatsiia* (nativisation) was developed by the Soviet authorities. The idea behind nativisation was that by drawing native cadres into the party their loyalty to other groups and Islam would be undermined. Despite the nativisation drive, by 1927 only about 40% of the Uzbek Communist Party were natives. Moreover, the aim of fostering new loyalties amongst the native elite was not achieved, instead the policy succeeded in drawing other identities into the party.

In the late 1920s, tensions between the native elites and the central authorities emerged in a variety of forms. Faizullah Khojaev, a veteran *Jadid*, head of the government of the People's Republic of Bukhara (1922–24) and chairman of the Council of People's Commissars of Uzbekistan (1924–37), opposed the development of the cotton monoculture in Uzbekistan. At the same time, a range of radical policies aimed at changing the culture of the region launched by the Soviet authorities further alienated the nationalist elite. Policies including the emancipation of women, the assault on Islam and collectivisation together broke the alliance that had been forged between nationalists and communists at the beginning of the decade.

With political allegiance and centralisation the order of the day, the policy to recruit representatives of the indigenous population into the Party was replaced by purges. In the period 1930–38 seven successive purges meant the arrest and execution of most of the nationalist leaders in Uzbekistan. Faizullah Khojaev was arrested in July 1937. The centrepiece of the purges was a showtrial in which first Secretary of the Communist Party of the UzSSR Akhmal Ikramov and Faizullah Khojaev were tried alongside Nikolai Bukharin, a leading figure of the so-called 'Right Deviation' in the Communist Party in 1938 and found guilty. Following the execution of Khojaev and other nationalist leaders, three successive Uzbek premiers were ousted in less than a year.

In place of the nationalist leaders a new generation of Soviet technocrats took control in Uzbekistan from the late 1930s, although Russians were also appointed (either local or 'parachuted' into key positions from Moscow). In the post-war period, Moscow continued and expanded its efforts to develop a new generation of local but loyal personnel. In particular, education was expanded in the republic to provide the specialists needed to fill important positions in Uzbekistan. As a result, the representation of titular groups in communist party organisations grew rapidly in the period 1945–1970, rising from 42.7% to 54.9%.

From the moment of the Soviet conquest of Central Asia, the central authorities were faced with a dilemma about personnel policies in the region. The problem for the Soviet authorities was that while Moscow wanted increased native representation there was a danger that as the number of locals rose they would import into the Communist Party patterns of behaviour from traditional society. By the Brezhnev era traditional regional and family alliances had come to underlay the internal politics of the republican Communist Party in many areas of Uzbekistan. Donald Carlisle has highlighted the struggle for power in Uzbekistan between a pro-Moscow Tashkent-Fergana elite and one composed of representatives from Samarkand and Bukhara. Ultimately under the leadership of the Samarkand-Bukhara group, particularly first Party Secretary Sharaf Rashidov (1959–83), the elite in the UzSSR gained from Moscow considerable discretion to act.[5]

Moscow's aim of extending its control over Uzbekistan through personnel policy was supported by initiatives designed to effect cultural transformation of the region. In the early years of the Soviet period, ambitious plans for transformation had to be curtailed for lack of resources and personnel and the need to conciliate the local elite and population. As a result, traditional courts were allowed some role in civil affairs and many local cultural patterns continued unchallenged.

There were, however, some changes designed to support the policies of fostering nations in Central Asia. In particular, the formation of the UzSSR was accompanied by the creation of an important set of national symbols. National histories were established and history written so that Russian conquest of the region was presented as a progressive development because it brought capitalism and Russian culture to Central Asia.

Most significantly, a popular and standardised new literary language was created in Uzbekistan. In the 1920s, the Arabic script was replaced by a Latin one designed to facilitate the emergence of a distinct Uzbek language. Language reform and Latinisation of alphabets in the late 1920s also served to limit the power of clerical groups still promoting religion through the Arabic script. The promotion of a single national language was also a powerful weapon in the struggle with the regions of Uzbekistan, many of which retained their own local dialects. In 1940 the Uzbek Latin script introduced in the late 1920s was changed to a Cyrillic script. The adoption of the Russian alphabet made obsolete millions of books printed in Latin and made the population semi-illiterate again.

From the late 1920s, a series of campaigns began which were to have a fundamental impact upon the society in Uzbekistan. In March 1927 *khudzhum* (advance) was launched in an effort to encourage female emancipation. In public ceremonies women removed their veils and burnt them. In the first two months of the campaign 9,000 women are reported to have broken traditional dress codes. The other campaign launched in the late 1920s, which was closely related to the women's liberation campaign, was the assault on Islam. During the following decade, Soviet anti-religious campaigns led to the closure of Muslim institutions (courts, schools and mosques) and the imprisonment and execution of many of the clergy.

The onset of World War Two eased the pressure placed upon Islam by the Soviets. In 1943 the Muslim Board of Central Asia was founded in Tashkent as part of the improving attitude towards religion; in the same decade two religious colleges and a small number of mosques were allowed to open in Uzbekistan. However, the assault on Islam was renewed under Khrushchev (1958–64) with the closure of mosques and reduction in the number of clergy. Under Brezhnev the anti-religious campaigns were moderated but from the late 1970s renewed moves were initiated against religion as a result of the resurgence of Islam in Afghanistan and Iran.

Advances in education were a central element in the drive to transform society in Uzbekistan. Education was the means by which the position of women was to be changed and traditional values, especially religious values, transformed. The means to achieve these aims was the imposition of a universal and secular education system in Uzbekistan. The introduction of universal compulsory education quickly raised the rate of literacy. Between 1926 and 1932 literacy rose from 3.8% to 52.5%. Education statistics were especially impressive with regard to raising the literacy of Muslim women.

The Soviet education system also helped to redress the imbalance in opportunities between the Slavic migrants and the local population. In the long term, the system led to the creation of a native scientific and technical elite, such that by 1975 57.6% of the total scientific/

technical intelligentsia in Uzbekistan were drawn from the native population.

After Stalin's death the cultural pressure on the Soviet Muslims was somewhat relaxed. The more benign cultural environment coupled with new opportunities created by the educational system and the rising power of the Uzbek political elite produced a cultural intelligentsia with a rising national self-consciousness. The 1960s were marked by a growing interest among the Central Asian Muslim intelligentsia in their national past. The 1970s saw the appearance of historical novels in Uzbekistan such as *The Treasure of Ulugbek* by Abil Yaqubov. This movement was to have an important impact upon the nationality politics of the *perestroika* period.

Alongside personnel and socio-cultural policies, the Soviet policies also had an important impact on the economic life of Uzbekistan. In the years after 1917, revolution and civil war critically damaged the republican economy and promoting economic regeneration became an important goal of the Soviet authorities. Initially, there was little in the way of radical economic policy in Uzbekistan, but in the late 1920s the pace of change accelerated dramatically. From the 1940s to the 1960s, the rise in industrial production in Central Asia as a whole outstripped the rest of the USSR. Despite the policy of state-led industrialisation, agriculture remained at the core of Moscow's vision for Uzbekistan.

The development of cotton production was promoted strongly by the Soviets, especially by Stalin. With the onset of World War Two, however, the production of food became more pressing and the area set-aside for cotton production declined. During the late 1940s cotton once again emerged as the dominant crop. By the late 1970s, Central Asia produced 95% of the USSR's cotton and fibres. In Uzbekistan the 'white gold' accounted for 65% of republican output and employed around 40% of the population.

The practice of taking more than 90% of the cotton crop to other parts of the USSR for processing distorted domestic economic production in Uzbekistan. The increase in cotton lands was closely connected with the decrease in the area occupied by grains, especially by rice, despite the fact that rice constitutes the major component in the local diet. Thus, the cotton monoculture also created a dependency on other republics for foodstuffs. Moreover, cotton requires much more irrigation than cereals, draining the scarce water resources of the region and exacerbating environmental problems.

Industrial development in Uzbekistan is of relatively recent origin. Prior to the October 1917 Revolution, there was little in the way of industry in the region. Agriculture was the dominant activity in the region under Stalin, however, the five year plans, wartime transplants of several large enterprises and the post-war programme of industrialisation helped alter the character of many parts of the region.

In the initial decades of Soviet rule, there was a steady growth of industrial infrastructure and an expansion of major urban centres, driven primarily by Slavic/European immigration. Economic growth continued after World War Two with the help of industry transferred from areas in the USSR threaten by Nazi invasion. Most of the Republic's population, however, continued to live a traditional rural way of life untouched by Soviet policies of modernisation, except for the dramatic expansion of cotton production initiated by Stalin.

In the 1970s the Central Asian economies began to face problems as capital investment failed to keep up with demographic growth and the population turned increasingly to the private sector and illegal and black-market activity flourished. Despite the best efforts of the Soviet planners the burgeoning native population largely refused to move to the towns and into industrial production, creating increased pressure on land and water resources.

Between 1917 and the mid-1980s, Soviet Uzbekistan made important socio-economic advances in the spheres of literacy, education, infant mortality, and health care. Despite these successes, the majority of the population remained rural, poor and infant mortality remained higher than in most other parts of the USSR. Although modern forms of economic activity and urban centres were developed, agriculture and in particular the cotton monoculture dominated the economic life of the Republic. In effect, the republican economy was based upon an ethnic division of labour, with Slavs/Europeans dominating industrial production and the native population confined to agriculture.

The Soviet policies to transform Central Asian societies also enjoyed mixed success. The Soviet state destroyed traditional institutions in many areas and introduced secular education and lifestyles. The Uzbek Republic was created and the Uzbek nation was granted official recognition and given the trappings of a nation including a history, language, and national symbols. At the same time, a Russian inspired vision of the world and its history was embedded in Uzbekistan and the use of Russian as a lingua franca was promoted.

Despite Soviet policies of repression and transformation, Muslim traditions and rites continued to be observed, especially in rural areas. In many locations, the apparent destruction of traditional society led only to its reappearance in other forms. Despite the drive to create secular nations and provide them with formal languages, cultures and administrative structure, sub-national identities continued to be important. Indeed, in the latter decades of the Soviet era, the identities of region, family, tribe, clan and religion seemed to acquire a new importance.

The most significant product of the Soviet period was the creation of the concepts of an Uzbek homeland, an Uzbek nation and all of appearance of an Uzbek national identity. The emergence of these ideas and their interlinking was both the product of deliberate policies and the by-product of broader socio-economic and cultural change in Uzbekistan.[6] Beneath the veneer of Sovietisation and Russification, national identity grew steadily within Uzbekistan and despite the apparent growth of Russian language usage in everyday life, the use of Uzbek continued. Significant divisions existed between the European/Slavic settlers and the native population and intermarriage between the two groups was rare. At the same time, Uzbek society remained split between different and competing regional groups.[7]

PERESTROIKA

In 1959, Sharaf Rashidov became first Secretary of the Communist Party of Uzbekistan and he stayed in office until his death in October 1983. In the 1960s and 1970s, there was a strong emphasis on stability amongst personnel within the Soviet system. As a result of this stability, Rashidov and the other provincial party bosses gained extensive powers. Under Rashidov's patronage a powerful political and economic order developed in Uzbekistan. Rashidov's ability to control this system provided the basis for republican elite to develop considerable autonomy from Moscow. The appointment of Yurii Andropov as General Secretary of the Soviet Communist Party and Rashidov's death in 1983 marked the onset of important changes in the political-economy that had evolved in the Republic during previous decades.

Under Andropov, a far-reaching purge of the Uzbek political establishment was launched. Ultimately the purge was to last for five years (1983–89). The purge was aimed at breaking the local networks of power that had built up in the course of the previous twenty-five years. Moscow's drive to 'de-Rashidovise' the republic served to bring a new generation of Uzbek leaders to the fore.

In 1983 a major fraud was revealed in the Uzbek cotton industry involving some 3,000m roubles. As the scandal developed it was used by the authorities in Moscow to discredit much of the political elite in Uzbekistan. With Gorbachev's ascent to the position of General Secretary, the cotton scandal became a cause celebre of the early *perestroika* years. While the official justification for the inquiry continued to be the drive to root out corruption, Moscow also used the issue to help in Gorbachev's programme to recentralise political control in the Soviet Union.[8]

Eventually, the cotton scandal led to the removal from office of the Uzbek Party leader Inamzhon Usmankhozhayev (January 1988), the Chairman of the Uzbek Supreme Soviet, Akil Salimov, and the Party leaders in Bukhara and Samarkand. The Moscow-inspired purge in Uzbekistan also focused on the role of Rashidov in fostering political and economic corruption. The denunciation of Rashidov and his regime thus became a central part of Moscow's assault on the Uzbek Communist Party in the 1980s.

The attack on the Brezhnev era elite in Uzbekistan was accompanied by the elevation of new leaders initially seen as loyal to Moscow and owing their promotion to Gorbachev. There were, however, also key events that intervened to trigger these developments. In June 1989 more than 100 people died in riots resulting from conflict between ethnic Uzbeks and members of the minority Meskhetian Turk community. The bloody ethnic riots in Fergana Valley altered Moscow's stance toward Uzbekistan. The centrally directed purge of cadres was moderated and Islam Karimov was appointed leader, replacing Rafik Nishanov. Karimov gradually began to rehabilitate the disgraced Rashidov.

In February-March 1990 there were further outbreaks of inter-ethnic conflict in Uzbekistan, culminating in three deaths during confrontations between police and demonstrators in Parkent, near Tashkent. In March 1990, the new Supreme Soviet convened. A leading member of the Uzbek political elite, Shakrulla Mirsaidov, was elected Chairman of the Council of Ministers. On 24 March 1990 Islam Karimov, first Secretary of the CPUz since 1989, was elected to the new position of executive President of the Republic by the Supreme Soviet at the first session of the Supreme Soviet; Shakurulla Mirsaidov was elected Chairman of the Council of Ministers.

Ethnic tension continued to rise in the region and in June 1990 clashes between Uzbeks and Kyrgyz in the Osh district of Kyrgyzstan threatened the stability of the whole Fergana Valley region. A state of emergency was declared in the Andizhan district on the Uzbek side of the border. In November 1990 the Council of Ministers was abolished and replaced by the Cabinet of Ministers under the leadership of the President; the position of Prime Minister ceased to exist and Mirsaidov was appointed to the new position of Vice-President.

Karimov's ascent to the highest office in Uzbekistan was achieved as many of the changes generated by the policies of the *perestroika* period began to sweep Uzbekistan. In October 1989 legislation was adopted that made Uzbek, rather than Russian, the official state language. On 20 June 1990, following the example of many other Soviet republics, Uzbekistan passed a declaration of sovereignty.

During the *perestroika* period, a number of new political groups appeared in Uzbekistan. The desiccation of the Aral Sea and the general deterioration of the environment caused by over-irrigation of land for cotton production served to mobilise ecological groups. As nationalist movements developed in the USSR as a whole, the status of Uzbek language became an important issue. In November 1988 a group of intellectuals founded *Birlik* (Unity), the first significant movement of opposition to the Communist Party of Uzbekistan. *Birlik* campaigned for a range of political and nationalist goals but its candidates were denied registration in the February 1990 elections to the Uzbek Supreme Soviet. During 1990, a further opposition party, *Erk* (Freedom) was created.

On 25 March 1989 *Birlik* failed in its attempt to put forward a candidate in elections to the Congress of People's Deputies of the USSR, having previously been refused official registration. On 18 February 1990 members of *Birlik* were prevented from standing as candidates in elections to the Uzbek Supreme Soviet; in many constituencies CPUz candidates were elected unopposed.

In April 1991, an overwhelming majority in Uzbekistan voted in favour of a 'renewed federation' during the all-union referendum on the future of the USSR. In the month following the referendum, Uzbekistan and eight other Union Republics agreed to sign a new Union Treaty in the summer of 1991. The intervention of the August coup in Moscow undermined this agreement. Once the coup collapsed, an extraordinary session of the Supreme Soviet declared the UzSSR independent; the Republic of Uzbekistan.

CONCLUSION

In historical terms Uzbekistan is a very new political formation, while even the appearance of the Uzbek nation and the minority communities within Uzbekistan are recent developments. Modern Uzbekistan and its population are, nevertheless, bound to the past in numerous ways. While many of these connections are often more imagined than real, the past exerts a powerful grip on the present. Since independence the pre-colonial past has been rediscovered, re-interpreted and bound to the present, often in unpredictable ways. Even the Soviet period has been subject to revisions that have abstracted a national narrative from the Communist period, complete with national heroes and villains.

In an environment when the tectonic plates of Central Asia history are in constant motion, divining a definitive history of the territories and populations of Transoxiana is problematic. Key historical figures, places and dates are perhaps not disputed, but their significance and interpretation are highly contested. While it may be difficult to fix a detailed single history of the region, the broad historical contours of Transoxiana can be sketched.

The Uzbekstani state and society are the contemporary descendants of a long line of political and socio-economic systems in Central Asia. Historically, the Uzbekistani territories have stood at the centre of a number of great empires and civilisations. Control of the region contained within the modern Uzbekistani state has also been critical for the ability of empires centred outside Central Asia to consolidate control over central Eurasia. The historical significance of Transoxiana gave it a political importance that was recognised and reflected in Soviet policies towards the region.

Historically, the geopolitical importance of Transoxiana has ensured that a variety of cultural influences and social forms have affected the region. While the Soviet regime sought to refashion the population of the region as socialist men and women, such aims were only rarely achieved. Instead, pre-Revolutionary cultures, religions, and identities survived the Soviet period, though changed in important and subtle ways. The Soviet project of modernisation did, however, alter the Transoxiana region in fundamental ways, although not always in the directions that Soviet planners intended.

The principal development of the Soviet period was the creation of the Uzbek national community and the proto-Uzbekistani state. The Soviets thus provided the cornerstones for the post-Soviet order.

Ethnic and national identities were developed and moulded during the Soviet period through conscious policies and as the by-product of urbanisation, the development of new forms of communication, and the myriad of other changes that accompanied the limited modernisation of the region effected by Moscow.

On the eve of independence, the political and socio-economic order in Uzbekistan was in flux. While much of traditional society remained intact, especially in the rural areas, new ideas and identities were developing in strategic sections of society, notably the political elite and cultural intelligentsia. The disintegration of the Soviet order accelerated many of the processes of transformation and propelled Uzbekistani society in new directions. The challenge of the post-Soviet leadership was to harness the new dynamics released within Uzbekistan in the late 1980s and reshape them into the basis for a new political and socio-economic order.

1 Edward A. Allworth, *The Modern Uzbeks: From the Fourteenth Century to the Present. A Cultural History* (Stanford, California: Hoover Institution Press, 1990).
2 Allworth, *Ibid.*, (1990), pp. 11–12.
3 Edward Allworth, ed., *130 Years of Russian Dominance, A Historical Overview* (London: Duke University Press, 1994).
4 Donald S. Carlisle, 'Soviet Uzbekistan: State and Nation in Historical Perspective' in Beatrice F. Manz, ed., *Central Asia in Historical Perspective* (Cambridge, MA: Harvard University Press, 1994), pp. 103–26.
5 Donald Carlisle, 'The Uzbek power elite: Politburo and Secretariat (1938-83)', *Central Asian Survey*, vol. 5, no. 3 (1986), pp. 109–18.
6 Bert G. Fragner, 'The Nationalization of the Uzbeks and Tajiks', in Andreas Kappeler, Gerhard Simon, and Georg Brunner, eds., *Muslim Communities Reemerge: Historical Perspectives on Nationality, Politics, and Opposition in the Former Soviet Union and Yugoslavia* (London: Duke University Press, 1994), pp. 13–32.
7 Demian Vaisman, 'Regionalism and Clan Loyalty in the Political Life of Uzbekistan', in Yaacov Ro'i, ed., *Muslim Eurasia: Conflicting Legacies* (London: Frank Cass, 1995), pp. 105–22.
8 James Critchlow, 'Corruption, Nationalism, and the Native Elites in Soviet Central Asia', *The Journal of Communist Studies*, vol. 4, no. 2 (June 1988), pp. 142–61.

Chapter 2

CONTEMPORARY POLITICS

INTRODUCTION

During the August 1991 anti-Gorbachev putsch, President Karimov failed to make his position on events in Moscow clear, although it is widely assumed that he was supportive of the action against the Soviet President and he may even have had connections to the coup plotters. In any event, Karimov did not condemn the putsch in Moscow until it became apparent it had failed. With the collapse of the coup, however, Karimov moved quickly to embrace independence for Uzbekistan. On 31 August, the Republican Supreme Soviet voted to declare the Uzbek SSR independent and on the following day the country's name was changed to the Republic of Uzbekistan. At the demise of the USSR, the Karimov regime lacked a defined strategy to carry the country forward. With independence suddenly thrust upon the republic, however, the government quickly adopted a set of domestic policies built upon the twin pillars of stability and consolidating Uzbek independence.

Karimov has argued, in particular, that the domestic and international circumstances that Uzbekistan finds itself in following independence, means that the first step in any process of change must be establishing stability throughout Uzbek society and in neighbouring states. Only on the basis of stability will reform have any chance of success. Further, the Uzbekistani President has promoted the idea that stability is premised upon further fostering Uzbek independence. The President has thus sought to bind the country together through an increased stress on a common identity and also to sever many of the external relationships of the past, particularly dependence upon Russia.

In practice, these twin aims have been pursued through a four-fold set of policies. First, the creation of a single system of power based around the institution of the presidency and the person of Islam Karimov. Second, a set of initiatives designed to forge a strong centralised state and to assert Tashkent's control over the regions. Third, the Uzbekistani leadership has promoted Uzbek nationalism as a means to unite society. Fourth, the government has been careful to suppress the development of all potential sources of opposition, particularly Islam.

Together, these policies have produced a highly authoritarian regime hinged upon the almost unlimited powers of the president. President Karimov has made ruthless use of the security forces to crush opposition and the media are tightly controlled by the state. Beneath a thin veneer of democratic practices and institutions, political power is wielded in an indiscriminate and unchecked fashion. The regime actively suppresses independent individuals and organisations, specifically targeting opposition and religious groups. Potential rivals to Islam Karimov within the regime are kept at bay through regular cycles of purges. At the same time, Uzbekistani society is being remoulded around a vision of Uzbekistan as a nation-state based upon a unitary state system and a strong Uzbek national community.

ISLAM KARIMOV AND THE PRESIDENTIAL SYSTEM

Following the collapse of the Soviet system, Islam Karimov emerged as the single most powerful political figure in the Republic of Uzbekistan. Despite the extensive powers that were available to Karimov, there were nevertheless important challenges to the President's position in the early 1990s. A number of potential challengers to Karimov were actively engaged in the republic's political life, while a range of political movements threatened the monopoly of power enjoyed by the formerly communist elite. In response to these challenges, and in the name of stability, one of the defining characteristics of Uzbekistani domestic politics since independence has been Karimov's drive to consolidate political power in the office of the President and the person of the incumbent. Simultaneously, the Karimov regime has been actively engaged in the systematic eradication of all forms of opposition to the regime, both at home and abroad.

To achieve these aims, political institutions other than the Presidency have been weakened and subordinated to Karimov. A set of pseudo-democratic institutions has been established, but behind this facade the president has de facto almost unlimited powers. Since independence the coercive activities of the Uzbekistani state have been considerably enhanced, opposition parties and leaders eradicated, and the media have been placed under tight government control and censorship. Many of these actions have attracted criticism from international human rights organisations. Alongside the relentless concentration of power in the hands of Karimov and the expansion of coercion and the activity of the security services, there have been constant efforts to prevent the development of powerful individuals or coalitions within the ruling elite capable of challenging Karimov's position. Thus, while society has been held in check by the state, the political elite has been kept in a state of almost constant flux, except for the President himself.

The creation of a system of one-man rule based upon Islam Karimov has involved four main elements: the establishment of a powerful presidential system of rule; the eradication of opposition; tight control over the media; and a near continuous purging of members of the political elite.

The Presidency

Islam Karimov became first Secretary of the Uzbek Communist Party in 1989 following ethnic rioting in the Fergana Valley. In March 1990, the Supreme Soviet elected Karimov to the newly established post of executive President. On 21 December 1991, following the demise of the USSR, Karimov was re-elected President but this time by a national popular vote; he is reported to have received 86%. The only other candidate, the Chairman of *Erk* (Muhammad Salih), received 14% of the vote. The leading opposition movement *Birlik* was not permitted to put a candidate forward for election as it lacked official registration as a political party. On the same day as the presidential election, 98.2% of voters backed independence for Uzbekistan in a referendum. Uzbekistan's sovereignty had, however, already been effected by the declarations of independence made by republican leaders and Gorbachev's resignation earlier in the month, which had dissolved the USSR.

The period following the declaration of independence was characterised by a political 'thaw' that lasted until the election of Karimov as president in December. Karimov had yet to achieve an unchallenged position in the republic and one month after the declaration of independence, about 200 deputies supporting the Vice President Shakrulla Mirsaidov, signed a letter critical of Karimov's dictatorial position.[1] Although restrictions were placed upon opposition groups, particularly in the run up to the presidential elections, movements such as *Birlik* were able to operate with a certain degree of freedom. The relatively benign environment also saw the emergence of new groups, such as the two religious-based parties *Islam Lashkari* (Islamic forces) and *Adolat* (Justice) which appeared in the Namangan district of the Fergana Valley and were active until March 1992.

Following the election of Karimov, the 'thaw' was ended quickly as the president moved to consolidate his position. Throughout 1992 the

People's Democratic Party of Uzbekistan (the former Communist Party) played the leading role in the political life of the country. President Karimov's rule became increasingly authoritarian. On 8 January 1992 the post of Vice-President was abolished and Karimov's main challenger Shakrulla Mirsaidov was, thereby, removed from office. Mirsaidov was appointed State Secretary, but soon resigned. He was later accused of financial improprieties. The post of Prime Minister (Chairman of the Cabinet of Ministers) was restored. At the same time, the government used the onset of civil war in neighbouring Tajikistan as justification for a further concentration of power and for repression of opposition movements, especially Muslim groups.

Since January 1992 the President has been able to exercise his control over the country's twelve regions (*viloyat*) through the establishment of the post of regional governor (*khokim*), which are appointed by the President. The *khokim* are prefects with extensive powers. The system of the *khokim* has played a leading role in the new system of local government that was set in place in the Republic. In particular, the construction of a powerful vertical system of executive power based upon the President's power to appoint regional governors has been closely tied to the centre's ability to control the local councils of people's representatives. Karakalpakstan, an autonomous republic within Uzbekistan, has its own president and in theory the region has the right to secede from Uzbekistan following a referendum. In fact, as with the other regions the Karakalpak president is appointed by and subordinated to Tashkent.

Additionally, the government also sought to promote the *mahalla*, or neighbourhood, as the basic element of local government. The *mahalla* was traditionally the basic unit of local organisation. The Karimov regime has revived the *mahalla* system, by giving the *mahalla* the status of 'organs of local government' in the constitution and a 1993 law. *Mahalla* have been created in towns and cities, and chairmen (*aksakal*) elected in each locality. In the countryside, the rural settlements are known as *kishlak*. Larger *kishlak* may also be sub-divided into *mahalla*. Although the government is keen to promote the idea that the *mahalla* system has served as a means to offer assistance to families, it also performs an important function of social control and has been used to extend the centralised authoritarian system down into each locality.

On 8 December 1992, the extensive powers of the President were formalised when the Supreme Soviet adopted a new Constitution. The

Constitution confirmed the President of the Republic as head of state. In the Constitution, Uzbekistan is declared a secular and democratic republic, and freedom of expression and religion are guaranteed for Uzbekistan's citizens. Plans were also announced for a new parliament to replace the Supreme Soviet as the highest legislative body following elections to be held in 1994.

On 22 September 1994 the Supreme Soviet met for the final time. In December, a 250-seat unicameral legislative body known as the *Oliy Majilis* replaced the old parliament. As a result of elections to the new parliament conducted on 25 December 1994, 144 of the 250 seats in parliament went to candidates nominated by regional councils (84 of these mayors or regional bosses). Overall, the People's Democratic Party (the ex-Communist Party) took 193 seats, while the remaining 57 seats were allocated to government supporters. Eighty percent of the *Oliy Majilis* was made up of representatives from institutions under the president's direct patronage. The *Oliy Majilis* thus emerged as a Soviet style institution that meets only every few months to approve laws prepared by the government.

Although there are a number of political parties active in Uzbekistan, in fact with the exception of the People's Democratic Party of Uzbekistan (PDPU), none of these parties has any significant function. In November 1991, having previously voted to sever links with the Communist Party of the Soviet Union, the Communist Party of Uzbekistan was renamed the People's Democratic Party of Uzbekistan. Initially, this organisation served an important role in mobilising support for the development of a system of one-man rule, however, in recent years as the Presidency has become the leading political institution, and the role of the PDPU has diminished considerably. In June 1996 Karimov left the PDPU, justifying his decision with the assertion that only a non-partisan head of state could serve as a guarantor of the constitution.

Besides the PDPU, there are four other officially registered political parties. These parties were created either by direct order or on the advice of the president and his government. In February 1995, *Vatan Taraqqiyoti* (Progress of the Homeland), which had been founded in May 1992 and was a pro-government party, was joined by a new 'official' or 'pocket' party (an organisation known for its pro-government, non-combative character) called *Adolat* Social Democratic Party of Uzbekistan. The new party was created when 47 deputies of the Popular Democratic Party (the former Communists) were drafted to provide a parliamentary membership for the party. In May 1995 two more 'official' parties were established, the National Revival Democratic Party (*Milli Tiklanish Demokratik Partisi*) and the People's Unity Movement (*Khalq Birliki*).

While the creation of pro-government parties has been one element of the drive to co-opt and control political expression in Uzbekistan, a ban on other forms of political organisation has formed the second element of political control. On 7th January 1997 a new law on political parties came into force.[2] The law specifically prohibits parties based upon religious or ethnic affiliations. Parties qualify for legal registration if they enlist at least 5,000 adherents from at least eight of the country's 14 regional-level administrative units. These provisions are clearly aimed at reinforcing the secular state, and forestalling a possible emergence of political Islam through the use of mosque buildings for political purposes. The law is also intended to stop regional or ethnic secessionist movements being able to organise politically.

At its first session in February 1995, the new parliament unanimously voted to hold a national referendum to approve an extension of the President's term. On 26 March 1995, 99.6% of the eligible electorate turned out for the referendum and 99.3% of these voted to extend President Karimov's term in office to 2000. The next parliamentary elections are scheduled for 1999, to be followed by a Presidential election in 2000. The constitution currently restricts the President to two terms of office, but revisions to this limit cannot be ruled out.

As a result of the political changes since independence, a system of one-man rule has been established in Uzbekistan. The President enjoys extensive powers including appointments and he resides at the pinnacle of a system of executive power that runs throughout the country and effectively subordinates all aspects of political life to its elements. The president takes all major, and many minor, decisions. Legislative power is dominated by executive power, while a range of pseudo-parties allegedly speak for the range of interests in Uzbekistani society.

The three most important institutions are the presidency, the National Security Service, and the Ministry of Agriculture and Water (because of the importance of the cotton crop and the large numbers involved in agricultural production). In many ways, the current system embodies the tradition of authoritarian rule that has dominated life in the region for centuries, however, the potential for unrestricted action and the resources available to the regime are greater than any of the previous systems.

Opposition movements and human rights

The construction of a system of one-man rule has been accompanied by the eradication of any potential opposition movements, particularly those that emerged in the period of limited *glasnost* from 1988 to mid-1992. One of the main aims of the government is to eliminate independent views and re-establish Soviet style fear and coercion, which weakened during the relatively liberal reform period of 1988–91. Throughout 1992, as the Uzbek leadership grew increasingly authoritarian, the activities of the opposition movements were restricted. A series of student demonstrations and the onset of civil war in neighbouring Tajikistan provided the pretext for the repression of all opposition organisations. The creation of a series of pseudo-democratic institutions including a parliament, political parties and organisations to protect human rights has provided the justification for the regime to crack down on 'unofficial' political organisations.

The assault on independent political forces has affected human rights in Uzbekistan negatively. In reality there is no freedom of media and almost no freedom of speech. Freedom of association and assembly is extremely limited, and there is practically no right of peaceful political or public activity. Through informants, infiltration, and other means, the police and security services have established extensive control on all aspects of public life, especially within the Islamic community. Freedom House has ranked Uzbekistan as one of the countries with the poorest record on democracy and human rights and classifies the country as a 'consolidated autocracy'.[3]

The main independent organisations are the *Birlik* (Unity) People's Movement and the associated *Birlik* Party (which began as the Democratic Party of Uzbekistan in June 1990 and adopted its current name in October 1991). The leading figure in *Birlik* is Abdurahim Polat. The *Birlik* movement and party promoted principles of independence, national rebirth, and a degree of democracy. The movement gained a broad popular following in the brief period of liberalisation in the period 1989–91. The *Birlik* movement was officially recognised on 12 November 1991 but the political wing of the movement was denied registration as a party. Several activists, notably Muhammad Salih, left *Birlik* and supported the Karimov government as the 'official opposition' in the form of the *Erk* party created in April 1990.

Salih emerged in republican politics in 1985 when he and his associates wrote a letter to Gorbachev to protest practices of the Uzbekistan government that undermined national cultural values. In 1988 Salih was elected Secretary of the Uzbekistan Writers' Union, which became the centre for unofficial opposition to the communist regime. The Union campaigned on issues of making Uzbek the state language, the environmental problems wrought by the communist regime, and the cotton monoculture. In 1989 Salih was closely involved in the foundation of the *Birlik* movement.

In the spring of 1992 *Erk* began to adopt a relatively more independent position. In July, after being denied the right to speak, *Erk* leader Salih resigned from parliament. The persecution of *Birlik* began in mid-1992. In June one of the movement's co-chairmen, Abdurahim Polat, was beaten by unknown assailants and less than a year later the other co-chairman was subject to the same experience. Throughout 1992–3, a number of opposition leaders disappeared or were assaulted. Many others were imprisoned.

As power was concentrated in the office of the President, opposition groups faced increased repression. On 1 October 1993 the government used technical pretexts to prevent both *Birlik* and *Erk* from registering with the Ministry of Justice; consequently both organisations were permanently banned. Two days later, *Erk's* newly elected first Secretary Samad Muratov, was assaulted by anonymous attackers. Polat and Salih fled the country. Both *Erk* and *Birlik* continue to operate from abroad and *Birlik* publishes the newspapers *Mustaqil Haftalik* (Independent Weekly), *Birlik* and the magazine *Harakat* (Movement).

As part of the government's political crackdown, conspiracy charges were issued against five *Erk* leaders living in exile since 1993, including the chairman Muhammad Salih and Jahongir Mamatov, the party's secretary and the editor of the *Erk* newspaper. In June 1994, two dissidents, Murod Zhorayev and Erkin Ashurov, were seized from their exile in Almaty in neighbouring Kazakhstan by an Uzbek security detail and taken to Uzbekistan to stand trial along with five other dissidents. On 31 March 1995 the Uzbekistan Supreme Court found the seven dissidents guilty of 'participating in a conspiracy to forcibly overthrow the constitutional government'. The trial was know as the *Erk* party trial, although there was in fact little direct connection to *Erk* party members. The government used this trial as part of an ongoing effort to discredit opposition groups by linking them with extremism or criminal activity. In this way, the Karimov regime has succeeded in reducing pressure from the international community over its human rights practice.

Despite the difficult political environment for opposition movements, some efforts to establish organisations to challenge the Karimov regime were still made. In the autumn of 1994, Shakrulla Mirsaidov and Ibrohim Boriev, at the time a prominent member of *Birlik*, helped launch the social democratic oriented *Haq Yol Adolat* (Justice is the True Way). This group was, however, unable to establish itself as a political organisation in Uzbekistan. In October 1995, opposition movements in Uzbekistan announced the creation of the Opposition Co-ordinating Centre in Tashkent. The Centre was led by Shakrulla Mirsaidov and was intended to bring together remnants of *Erk*, *Birlik*, and Mirsaidov's own party. Many Uzbek dissidents continue to be active abroad, notably in Russia, Turkey and the United States and *Birlik* conducted a conference in Moscow in July 1995.

In 1995 the government began attempts to change its image as one of the worst human rights violators among the former Soviet republics. Human rights activists were released, including the deputy chairman of *Birlik*. Human Rights Watch, the international human rights organisation, was permitted to undertake a fact-finding mission to Uzbekistan in November 1995. In July 1996, Human Rights Watch was also allowed to station a field representative in Tashkent.

In the summer of 1996 President Islam Karimov stated his intention to initiate democratic reforms. He also called for a free media and 'aggressive journalists' criticising the government bureaucracy. In September the Uzbekistani authorities allowed a conference of the Human Rights Society of Uzbekistan to be held in Tashkent, the first relatively free meeting of pro-democratic activists for years. The government also hosted an OSCE sponsored seminar on human rights, allowing about twenty independent activists, opposition representatives and members of the government's human rights practices.

In 1996, Abdurahim Polat was allowed to return from exile in the US and the best-known local dissident Shukrulla Mirsaidov was allowed to speak at a much publicised human rights conference. But by October the thaw was over and persecution of opposition, human rights, and Islamic activists resumed; restrictions on freedom of association were not removed, and restrictions on travel were restored. A new law on political parties introduced in January 1997 imposed even further obstacles for political party registration and 'justified' the government's continued full control over political life.

Persecution of Mirsaidov was resumed. Mirsaidov and his three sons were evicted from their homes and the authorities forced members of this extended family from their houses. The action was based upon on a 1993 Uzbekistan Supreme Court decision awarding the government $5.5 million because of supposed damages to the economy caused by Mirsaidov's 'misuse of power' as vice-president in 1990–91. Human Rights Watch has suggested that Mirsaidov has suffered assassination attempts through car bombings, beatings, kidnapping, threats and heavy surveillance.

An important factor that fostered the renewed emphasis on coercion was events in Afghanistan. The Taliban's advance at the time and fear that Uzbekistan would soon have a border with an Islamic state alarmed Karimov and his advisers. Much of the hope for positive change was also based on the apparent economic improvements during 1995 and early 1996, but the situation dramatically worsened after October. The state's cotton harvest, the country's largest export earner, was 20 percent below projections, causing a $400m loss in revenue. The poor harvest meant $300 million lost in grain exports. In this situation the government restricted the convertibility of local earnings into hard currency and prices and shortages increased sharply. The economic problems across the country caused concern in Tashkent that social unrest would follow and renewed efforts to control discontent.

Since 1996, political repression has continued. The opposition figures that fled abroad continue to have pressure placed upon them by the Karimov regime. Human Rights Watch has complained to President Karimov about the treatment of Muhammad Salih, who was expelled from Turkey on 15 November 1997 prior to Karimov's visit to Ankara. On 4th March 1998, Salih was again forced to leave Turkey prior to the visit of the Turkish Prime Minister Mesut Yilmaz to Uzbekistan. Relatives and friends of Salih have faced persecution in Uzbekistan. At a plenary session of the banned opposition party *Erk* in Tashkent at the end of November 1997, a letter to President Karimov was drawn up asking permission for the party chairman Muhammad Salih to be allowed to return.[4] In January 1998, Uzbek security forces crossed to neighbouring Kyrgyzstan, arrested the opposition figure Zakirjan Normatov in Osh, and took him to Tashkent without notifying the Kyrgyzstani authorities.

In the middle of 1996, the Uzbekistani government began to establish 'official' human rights organisations, much as pocket political parties had been established earlier. In April 1996, the post of human rights ombudsman was established in the parliament, but a regime loyalist was appointed to the position. The National Human Rights Centre of the Republic of Uzbekistan was created by Presidential decree in October 1996. The Centre opened in March 1997. Although initially greeted as opening a new era in Uzbekistan, these institutions have done almost nothing to improve the observation of human rights in the country.

Tashkent's efforts to establish a pseudo-human rights regime have helped to gain the country support from western countries. Not only has the United States eased its criticism of Uzbekistan since 1995, but the European Union (EU) has also moderated its position. In January 1996, the EU proposed starting negotiations on a Partnership and Cooperation Agreement (PCA) with Uzbekistan. Germany was apparently the leading country promoting the PCA. Despite high level support in the European Commission for a swift ratification of the PCA, the European Parliament has resisted passing and Agreement. In October 1997, the director of the OSCE Office for Democratic Institutions and Human Rights concluded a set of agreements with the Uzbekistani Foreign Minister on promoting democracy and developing civil society.[5]

Despite the limited relaxation on political activities launched in 1996, in March 1998 Shakrulla Mirsaidov, leader of the Democratic Opposition Co-ordinating Council, unexpectedly announced that the Council had formally ceased to function. He noted that it had been impossible to bring together all democratic forces in the country. Mirsaidov also said that the Uzbekistani government has 'laid down the foundations for establishing a democratic and legal state and implementing reform programme toward a free market'.[6]

Following a series of bomb blasts in Tashkent in February 1999, the Uzbekistan authorities launched a major campaign against all potential opposition organisations. Hundreds were arrested, tortured or simply disappeared. Leading critics of the regime in Turkey, Ukraine and central Asian states were extradited to face an uncertain future in Uzbekistan.

The media

The ability of the regime to control political events in Uzbekistan has been critically dependent upon the tight control and censorship exercised by the authorities over the media. Officially, from 1995 the government has supported a free media but, in fact, there has been a steady restriction on its activities. The constitution and laws explicitly forbid censorship, yet it continues to be widely practised. The problems of free speech and free media in Uzbekistan are not issues of harsh laws but of the way in which the laws are enforced.

The government of the Republic of Uzbekistan bears most of the responsibility for the development of a restrictive media regime, rather than as the government claims the pressures of the transition process. The Uzbekistani government is directly responsible for the perpetuation of censorship, firings, harassment and intimidation of journalists, and for creating an atmosphere that is so repressive that journalists often censor themselves. Journalists who deviate or attempt to deviate from the unwritten but universally understood limits of topics and tone, have been expelled from the country, fired from their jobs or threatened with dismissal. Journalists have on occasion been beaten or faced violence, and their families faced harassment by the security services.

Following the brief period of media liberalisation in the final years of the Soviet system and the immediate post-independence period, the Uzbekistan regime moved quickly to re-establish strict control. In December 1993, a compulsory re-registration of the mass media was announced as a result of which independent publications were outlawed.

Almost all media in Uzbekistan are owned by the state. The current Law on the Mass Media makes it extremely difficult to set up a private, independent newspaper. Article five of the law states: 'the right to found mass media belongs to Councils of People's Deputies and other state bodies, to registered political parties, public associations, mass movements, creative unions, and co-operatives, religious and other civic associations set up in accordance with the law, and to labour collectives.'

According to the government, in April 1998 there were 471 publications in Uzbekistan: sixty-six national newspapers, eighty-eight regional, and the remainder town and district periodicals. Despite the numbers, in reality Uzbekistan's print media are dominated by three national daily newspapers: the Uzbek and Russian language sister publications *Khalq Sozi* (People's Word) and *Narodnoe Slovo* and the Russian language paper *Pravda Vostoka* (Truth of the East). The weeklies represent a diversity of interests, ranging from the views of the various official political parties to economics, and the stock exchange.

Television and radio are generally more influential than the press. The Television and Radio company of Uzbekistan has four national television stations. The majority of programmes are in Uzbek, although there are also Russian language news bulletins. National Television carries some programme from Russian State Television. All of the television stations are under close government control.

Since 1995, leading western foreign news radio stations such as Radio Liberty, Voice of America and the BBC have been granted accreditation in Uzbekistan. Most western journalists have found it extremely difficult to operate in the country. Print and broadcast media emanating from the Russian Federation or affiliated to the Russian media have been restricted. The rebroadcasting of Russian programmes and the accessibility of Russian newspapers has declined markedly.

Personnel policy

One of the main strategies employed by the president to ensure his continuing political dominance has been a policy of regular personnel turnover among the political elite. This policy is intended to prevent the development of powerful political figures and coalitions that might challenge the president. The periodic dismissal of leading members of the government also gives the president a regular supply of people to blame for the country's problems.

Karimov made the most important change when he dismissed Mirsaidov, a former ally but also a potential threat to the president, from the position of vice-president in 1992. In 1994 and 1995, the President continued to strengthen his position. In the Summer of 1994, Mavlon Umurzakov, one of President Karimov's state councillors was removed, followed in July by a presidential decree dismissing the mayor of Tashkent, Adkham Fazylbekov, who had been a close associate of Mirsaidov.

On 21 December 1995, the Uzbekistani *Oliy Majilis* dismissed the Prime Minister Abdulkhosim Mutalov, a decision ostensibly prompted by economic difficulties, notably the fall in value of the national currency. With Mutalov's dismissal, President Karimov had removed most of the core of politicians who had helped him to power in the late 1980s, including Mirsaidov, the former Justice Minister and Ambassador to the US, Babur Malikov, and the former Foreign Minister Said-Mukhtar Saidkasimov. Mutalov was replaced with Utkur Sultanov, previously minister for foreign economic relations.

On 15 May 1997, the former finance minister Bakhtiar Hamidov was demoted. Hamidov was widely regarded as number two in the

Karimov administration and a possible successor to Karimov. Hamidov became the scapegoat for the ongoing balance-of-payments crisis. At the end of 1997, the failure of the cotton and grain harvest again produced a round of sackings of senior officials and public reprimands handed out by the president. The agriculture and defence ministers were replaced, as were a number of regional leaders. The agricultural minister Marx Jumaniyozov, was dismissed for allegedly forging data on the cotton harvest.

No reasons were given for the sacking of the defence minister, Colonel-General Rustam Ahmedov, who had served in that post since Uzbekistan gained independence. He was removed on the 29th September as the Taliban approached Uzbekistan's southern border. Ahmedov's replacement was from the border guards, suggesting the two events were linked. In November the President moved against his de facto number two in Uzbekistan, Ismail Jurabekov. Jurabekov controlled major sectors of the economy, including the countries main hard currency earner, the cotton trade. The removal of Jurabekov was viewed as a significant consolidation of Karimov's power. Perhaps reflecting Karimov's experience of the factional and clan politics of the Soviet era in Uzbekistan, the president has particularly targeted regional leaders for regular dismissal.

Control of the regions

Uzbekistan has a highly centralised form of decision-making. The main administrative units of the country, Uzbekistan's 12 *viloyat*, the city of Tashkent and the republic of Karakalpakstan, have little power. During the Soviet period, Uzbekistan's regions operated as important bases for establishing political networks.[7] The current leadership of Uzbekistan is dominated by personnel from the Samarkand-Jizzakh grouping (of which Karimov is the leading member) and is reportedly locked in a struggle for power with the Tashkent, Fergana-Namangan-Andizhan groupings.

Since independence almost all of the regional leaders have been subject to replacement. Beginning in 1995, the poor state of the economy and the weak harvest provided the pretext for the emergence of a pattern of regular dismissals of regional leaders. In 1996 four regional leaders lost their jobs. The final official to be removed was the *khokim* of Bukhara region, Mavlon Rakhmonov, who was dismissed on 14 December 1996 and replaced with the former Deputy finance Minister Samoydin Husenov.

The regional purge continued into 1997 with the removal of Mirzajon Islamov from his post as administrative head of the Fergana region on 14 February 1997. The president reportedly considered the pace of privatisation and economic reform in the area to have been too slow. His successor was named as Numonjon Mominov, a district head of administration from the same Fergana apparatus as Islamov. On 17 July 1997 Karimov visited the Karakalpak Autonomous Republic and told an extraordinary session of the local parliament that the region's leadership was responsible for a 'gigantic cash deficit'. Karakalpak parliamentary speaker Ubaniez Ashirbekov was sacked and replaced by an official recommended by Karimov.

The pattern has continued into 1998 with the sacking of the *khokim* of Navoi Region, Hayot Ghafforov, on 11 November 1998. Karimov announced the dismissal at an extraordinary session of the Navoi Regional Council of People's Deputies during a visit to this region. The former first deputy of Bukhara Region, named as Ghaybulla Odilov, was appointed as the new governor of the region.

The removal of regional figures has been an important element of the consolidation of the Karimov regime. The president has made strenuous efforts to prevent any regional leaders developing entrenched networks of power in their districts. Karimov has sought to replace the regional centred politics of the Soviet era, with the establishment of a national elite focused upon Tashkent. Any regional leader who fails or challenges central authority is sacked. Regional leaders have also provided a convenient group to blame when the harvest fails or the economy dips, deflecting attention from the failings of central government. Especially close control is exerted over Tashkent, the Fergana region, Samarkand and Bukhara.

NATIONALISM

A theme of growing significance in Uzbekistan has been the development of a national identity anchored upon Uzbek nationalism. Following independence, the Uzbekistani authorities launched a powerful top down drive based upon an essentially mono-ethnic vision of the nation-state, the official rhetoric about pluralism not withstanding. Significantly, the former communist leadership has sought to position itself as the champion of a restored Uzbek nation. The Uzbekistani state has promoted Uzbek culture and the writing of a national history, including fostering a cult around the historic figure Amir Timur. Since 1989 Uzbek language has received increased priority within Uzbekistan and in 1993 it was decreed that Uzbekistan would replace a Cyrillic with a Latin script. While many of these measures have helped to bind Uzbek society closer together, major questions about the place of minorities in the nation-building project remain.

Nation and elite

Since 1991 a new historiography has been used to justify official policies and state structures. Of particular importance have been efforts to bind the country's former Soviet elite to a nationalist interpretation of the past. This process has involved a rewriting of the biographies of many of the communist elite. The focus of the new history has been the so-called 'Class of 38' (those beneficiaries of purges of the late 1930s who went on to hold high office in the Communist Party of Uzbekistan and dominated political life in the republic from 1938–83).[8] In this new interpretation, the Class of 38 have been made into national heroes who struggled for the Uzbek, not the Soviet, nation. The new elite biographies have been a central element of official nationalism and have been used to develop a new legitimacy for the former communist elite in the aftermath of the 'Uzbek' or 'Cotton affair', which served to discredit the republican party.

Following independence, the communist elite in Uzbekistan faced a serious challenge to its hegemony. As Moscow's hold over the republic weakened, the Uzbek Communist Party was discredited as a result of the 'Cotton Affair', while the emergence of *Birlik* and *Erk* threatened to develop and open the political arena to other forces, thereby reducing the communist leadership's political dominance in the Uzbek SSR. In this environment, a means to relegitimise the party elite was required. To counter the rise of groups such as *Birlik*, *Erk* and the Islamic Renaissance Party, Karimov moved to co-opt much of the agenda of the opposition movements, particularly the nationalist elements which were repackaged in forms that linked the communist elite to Uzbekistani society in new ways.

With independence, much of the CPUz was transformed into the People's Democratic Party and the party elite moved to fill the vacuum of political power created by the weakening of the former Soviet centre. The key element of the new approach was the launch of an 'official nationalism' in which the former party leaders emerged as patriots protecting and promoting the Uzbek nation. The focus of this campaign was the former Uzbek leader Sharaf Rashidov.

The denunciation of Rashidov and his regime formed a central part of Moscow's assault on the Uzbek Communist Party in the latter 1980s. Following independence, Rashidov's rehabilitation became a priority for Uzbekistan's leadership. After 1991 Rashidov was presented as a national hero presiding over the rejuvenation of Uzbekistan. As part of this policy, streets throughout Uzbekistan were named after Rashidov and his statue was erected in the centre of Tashkent. At the same time, the two leaders who had worked with Moscow to discredit much of the CPUz, Inamjan Usmankhojaev (CPUz first Secretary from 3 November 1983 to 12 January 1988) and Rafik Nishanov (CPUz first Secretary 12 January 1988 until 23 June 1989), became the subjects of strong official criticism. *Birlik* opposed the rehabilitation of Rashidov and blamed him for the destruction of the Aral Sea. The promotion of official nationalism, however, allowed criticism of Rashidov by *Birlik* to be equated with betrayal of the homeland.[9]

Rewriting a national past

During the Soviet period nation-building came to be increasingly controlled by the communist authorities in Uzbekistan. As a result of Tashkent's increasing engagement with the national project, in the late 1980s a process of historical revision was undertaken by Uzbek historians. These historians rejected the standard Soviet interpretation of subjects such as the Jadid reformist movement, and refuted the view that Central Asia was united willingly with the Tsarist empire. They also developed a positive view of national resistance movements such as the *Basmachi* in the 1920s.

Following independence the new Uzbek government has been unwilling to relinquish the monopoly on history writing and many of the tendencies of the late Soviet period have been accelerated. Indeed, the Uzbek elite has harnessed historians to provide the national foundations of the independent state. A central element of the nation-building project in Uzbekistan has been a sustained effort to write and rewrite a specifically national history.

Within this project, Uzbeks are presented as an ancient civilisation on a par with other ancient civilisations along the Silk Road. Central Asian literary and scientific figures such as Berune, Navoi, and Ibn Sina are claimed as exclusively Uzbek. As part of the nation-building agenda monuments have been erected, and holidays and conferences organised to celebrate various historical figures as Uzbeks.[10]

As noted in the previous chapter, the origins of the Uzbeks and the date when the Uzbeks became a nation are disputed. Some historians suggest an Uzbek nation only came into existence in twentieth century, while most contemporary Uzbek historians suggest the Uzbeks originate many hundreds of years ago and possibly date from the first century BC or earlier. While it seems likely that the first reference to a group identified as Uzbek came with the Shaibanid conquest in the sixteenth century, the first efforts to foster a linguistic-based ethnic Uzbek identity on the model of European nations took place under the Soviet authorities.

One of the most notable elements of the reinvention of the past has been the programme by the Uzbekistani authorities to foster a cult around the figure of Amir Timur. Timur, the fifteenth century Turkic conqueror and empire-builder known in the West as Tamerlane, has emerged as the central icon of a campaign to rewrite national history and as part of the broader movement toward an Uzbek 'cultural renaissance'.[11] As early as the 1950s Soviet historians fixed Timur as a representative of a specifically Uzbek history, although he was identified as a destructive feudal conqueror. Independence in 1991 presented Uzbek historians with new opportunities and new challenges to dismantle the Soviet historiography. The rediscovery of Timur has involved three main elements. First, Timur has been established as a symbol of Uzbek national pride. Second, Timur has been identified as the ideal 'just ruler' and state builder, with his policies and methods providing historical justification for the policies and methods of the current Uzbek government. Finally, Timur has been promoted as the 'fountainhead' of Uzbekistan and an emblem of Uzbekistan's re-emergence as an independent regional power.[12]

In September 1993 President Karimov dedicated a statue to Timur on the site where a monument to Marx had previously stood in the centre of Tashkent. In his speech at the dedication, Karimov sought to draw out the continuities between Timur and the new Uzbek republic. The new Timur is, thus, the centrepiece of an Uzbek national ideology, based on the idea that the Uzbeks have been, since time immemorial, the dominant political and cultural force in Central Asia. Parallels have frequently been drawn between Karimov and Timur in the Uzbekistani press.

Language

In October 1989 the law 'On the State Language', which granted Uzbek the status of the state language within the Uzbek Socialist

Republic, was adopted. The law made Russian the language of inter-ethnic communication but required employees in the state sector to know Uzbek. In September 1993, the Supreme Council of the Republic of Uzbekistan decreed the replacement of the Soviet era Cyrillic script with a Latin one. Progress with the transformation of the language has been slow because of problems in developing a standard Latin script and a lack of resources.

In December 1995, a revised language law was passed. The new law no longer requires employees in the public sector to know Uzbek but has also abolished the special status Russian enjoyed under the 1989 law. The new law also makes no provision for the study of the Arabic script, which was in place until the 1920s and is still a potent symbol of Islam in the Republic.

At the core of the new language arrangements are issues of power and status rather than communication. Language is a symbol of group identity and power. In the future, Uzbek is clearly to be the dominant language in the republic. The demoted status of Russian reflects Uzbekistan's heightened independent stance in regard to the Russian Federation and CIS structures. There are still, however, numerous dialects of Uzbek in use in the country and Russian remains the lingua franca of many in the Uzbek elite. The demise of Russian has, nevertheless, bought differences between indigenous and Russian settler cultures into sharp relief.[13]

An important symbolic change has been the switch from Cyrillic to a Latin alphabet. While Cyrillic continues to be the leading alphabet for both Uzbek and Russian, there has been rapid shift over to the Latin script in cities in terms of street signs and official buildings. Russian has all but disappeared from many public spaces in the capital, Tashkent.

Minorities

A central issue affecting the prospects for the Uzbek nation-building project will be the reaction of Uzbekistan's minorities to the new regime and its policies. The official nationalism employed by the Uzbekistani authorities appears aimed to emulate the mono-ethnic nation-state model and so provides little space for non-Uzbeks. By exalting the Uzbek nation, the state is in danger of excluding the other communities resident in Uzbekistan. The significant minority populations in Uzbekistan, including Slavs, Tajiks, and the various groups submerged within the broader Uzbek identity (such as Kashgari, Kipchaks or Turks), suggests that a pluralist model would be a more appropriate strategy for the country.[14]

The population of Uzbekistan was estimated to be more than 23 million in 1995.[15] The titular nationality is over 17 million people but there are representatives of more than 100 nationalities in the republic. Besides Uzbeks, there are more than a million Tajiks and approximately the same number of Russians and Kazakhs, 420,000 Karakalpaks, up to 300,000 Tatars, about 200,000 Koreans, more than 170,000 Kyrgyz , over 150,000 Ukrainians, and approximately the same number of Turkmen. Uzbeks constitute a majority in all districts of the republic except for the nominally autonomous Karakalpakstan.[16]

During the years of Soviet power, the ethnic composition of the Republic of Uzbekistan underwent important changes. Since 1919, the titular population has risen from 3.5 million. There was also a dramatic rise in the Slavic population during the Soviet period as a result of economic development in Uzbekistan from the end of the 1920s, population evacuations during World War Two, and the development of large industrial projects in the 1950s. As a result of these migrations, urban centres such as Almalyk, Shargun, Uchkuduk, Chirchik, Angren, Navoi, and Zaravshan attained a Slavic population of up to 80–85%. The numbers of minorities in the republic was also swelled as a result of the deportation of the Crimean Tatars, the Meshketian Turks, Kurds, Germans, and Koreans in the 1930s and 1940s. Partly as a result of these changes, the proportion of the titular nationality in Uzbekistan decreased from 80% (in the pre-war period) to 70% in 1989.

In June 1989, the first widely publicised interethnic conflict broke out in Uzbekistan. The conflict involved Meshketian Turks and Uzbeks in the Fergana Valley. Economic decline in the region led to demands by the local Uzbeks to expel the 'foreigners' and 'strangers'. The growing tension engendered by economic decline and ethnic conflict also helped the emergence of the Islamic Revival Party. In March 1990, similar conflicts in the Buka and Parkent districts of Tashkent region, led to the departure of almost all of the Turkish population from the republic.

Although it has tended to be the smallest minority groups that have experienced the most violent treatment in Uzbekistan, official policies to support the Uzbek nation-building project raise important questions about the larger groups resident in the country. Of particular importance are the populations of Tajiks and Slavs.

Tajiks

A Persian-based culture has an ancient heritage in the oasis regions of Central Asia, and prior to Russian conquest Persian and Turkic civilisations were closely interlinked, if not fused, in many of the urban centres of present day Uzbekistan. It was Soviet nationality policies that created 'Uzbek' and 'Tajik' as separate ethnicities. This distinction was essentialised and institutionalised by decades of Soviet bureaucratic mechanisms.

The Soviet years are linked with a politicisation of ethnicity, and the demise of the centuries old Persian-based culture. Despite these changes, the Tajiks remain Uzbekistan's largest ethnic minority. Tajik populations are particularly important in the cities of Samarkand and Bukhara, where they constitute majorities. Tajiks are also found in the mountainous areas outside Tashkent, in the Fergana valley, Jizzakh province, Surkhan Daria and Kashka Daria.

As a result of the policies of the 1920s, in 1991 the Uzbek elite inherited a conception of Uzbek nationality and national borders established by Soviet planners, and it is these elements that have provided the basis for contemporary Uzbek nation-building policies. However, despite the best efforts of Soviet officials to construct separate ethnic identities based upon language, the distinction between Uzbek and Tajik is often blurred especially in areas where Tajiks are numerically superior.

Soviet census returns from the 1920s show that large numbers of Persian-speakers disappeared into the category of Uzbeks during the process of territorial delimitation. A recent book by the Tajik writer Rahim Masov has claimed that a 'process of genocide concerning the Tajik people' was initiated following the Soviet delimitation policies when two-thirds of the territory inhabited by Tajiks was incorporating within the Uzbek Republic.[17] He argues that with the key Tajik centres located in the Uzbek SSR following delimitation, the Persian-speakers were subject to assimilation and lost their identity as a consequence.

While it is clear that the category of Uzbek has been privileged by the changes instituted in the 1920s, it is not entirely accurate to suggest that the Tajiks have been assimilated against their wishes. An Uzbek identity has often served as an umbrella term containing a wide range of different groups. Many individuals move between different forms of ethnic self identification and large numbers of Uzbekistani Tajiks are officially registered as Uzbeks. Official census figures of the Tajik population are, therefore, likely to be misleading, and some have suggested that the figure might be closer to six million, or twice the number located in the nominal Tajik republic. The ambiguous nature of Tajik and Uzbek identity in many regions makes it impossible to say how many Tajiks there are in Uzbekistan.

In the last decades of Soviet rule, rising Uzbek national sentiment amongst sections of the republican elite led to measures to restrict official support for the Tajik population. From the middle of the 1960s education in Tajik was scaled down causing tension in Bukhara and Samarkand and the Tajik populated rural centres nearby. In the late 1980s, significant interethnic tension emerged between Tajiks and Uzbeks. In the middle of 1988 demonstrations took place in Samarkand and Bukhara with some participants demanding that territories with a Tajik majority be united with Tajikistan. It was reported that many of these actions were co-ordinated by the Tajik Liberation Front, a shadowy and small movement. A society of Uzbekistani Tajiks 'Samarkand' was formed, which has been led by U. Bekmuhamedov since 1991. The Uzbekistani authorities have, however, been anxious to prevent any unofficial organisation from emerging among the Tajiks.

Since independence, the position of the Tajiks has not improved. Efforts by Tajiks in Uzbekistan to expand Tajik-language education, publishing and television have largely been thwarted by the government. The Tajiks also appear to have been marginalised from the new areas of economic activity in the country, with Tajik run markets having a lower status than those run by Europeans and Uzbeks.[18] Tajiks also lack significant formal political representation at the highest levels.

Despite the aggressive nation-building policies of the Uzbekistani government, as yet there has been little violent confrontation between Tajiks and Uzbeks. As many Tajiks are bilingual, the new laws on language have had little affect upon them. The Tajiks are also accustomed to a minority status, since it was thrust upon them by the Soviets in the 1920s. Tajik culture has not flourished in Uzbekistan under the Soviets and appears destined to struggle in an independent Uzbekistan.

Slavs

A significant Slavic population emerged in Uzbekistan during the Soviet period, particularly attached to the programme of industrialisation and the construction of large urban areas. During the Soviet era, Slavs dominated important areas of the economy and they formed large communities in many of the leading cities and towns, notably Tashkent. Although there has been little in the way of direct confrontation between Uzbeks and Slavs, since independence, there has been a sizeable Slavic out-migration from the republic prompted by a general perception that the advantages that the Slavs had previously enjoyed were quickly disappearing.

The political fragmentation of the *perestroika* period allowed the rise of nationalist sentiments in the republic and often these took the form of anti-Russian sentiments. Interethnic tension first emerged at the end of the 1980s, although isolated instances of conflict were reported earlier. As early as May 1969 a football match in Tashkent led to fighting between Uzbeks and Russian-speakers. Rioting lasted for several days. One of the reasons for the anti-Russian rioting was the decision to distribute 20% of the flats being built in Tashkent to Russians who had come to reconstruct the capital after the earthquake of 1966. In the same period there were riots by the Crimean Tatars who wished to return to Crimea or gain some autonomy in Uzbekistan.

Following independence, there was a strong sense among the Russians that with Moscow no longer able to determine developments in Uzbekistan, the Slavs would be removed from their former leading positions. Many of these fears appear to have been substantiated with a rapid decline in the number of Russians in managerial and administrative positions. The previous over representation of Russian-speakers in many spheres has been reversed and now the Slavs are generally under represented in critical areas of political and economic life.

The Slavic population has been particularly alarmed by the new language law, which made Uzbek the official language of the country and greatly restricted the use of Russian. The decline in importance attached to Russian language and the necessity of knowing Uzbek threatens the position of the Slavic community in Uzbekistan. The constraints placed upon Russian-language mass media and fear about the future quality of education in the republic also cause concern.

The immediate response to independence by large sections of the Slavic population was emigration. In the first years of independence there was an exodus of Russian-speakers from Uzbekistan. About 100,000 Russians, Ukrainians, Germans and Jews left the republic annually in the early 1990s. This emigration threatened serious consequences to Uzbekistan because the Slavs constituted the majority of managers, scientists, technicians, teachers, and professionals. Fear of a 'brain drain' lead the Uzbekistani authorities to assure the Slavs that they would still have a future in the country.

A major question mark remains, however, over the Slavic population in Uzbekistan. Separated by cultural and religious differences, the Uzbek and Russian communities historically have lived as separate groups. Following independence, the vast majority of Slavs have continued to live in communities with little direct contact with Uzbeks. The majority of the Russian-speakers do not wish to learn Uzbek, or the traditions, culture, and customs of the country. Many Russians nevertheless appear to want to stay and to adapt to the new situation but not to assimilate to an Uzbek culture; rather to carry on as during the Soviet era. As a result, the Russian-speaking population of Uzbekistan does not feel integrated with Uzbek society. The lack of association with independent Uzbekistan makes it difficult for the Slavs to see themselves as citizens. At the same time, the Russian-speakers have kept a low political profile. There are no Russian-based political parties in Uzbekistan and the Russian-speakers have not put forward demands for political or cultural autonomy.

As well as Slavic emigration, there has also been a large exodus of Germans. In 1989 there were 40,000 ethnic Germans living in Uzbekistan but since then more than 15,000 have left for Germany. Sizeable numbers of Central Asian Jews have also left the republic, most for Israel. However, not all minorities wish to emigrate, have the opportunities to emigrate or have a homeland willing to except them. The Koreans, for example, have remained in Uzbekistan and are now engaged actively in commerce.

ISLAM

Since independence, Islam has become a particularly important issue in Uzbekistan. The government has actively sponsored a revival of Islam and President Karimov made the pilgrimage, or 'haj', to the holy sites in Mecca soon after he changed seamlessly from the republic's communist chief to become president of independent Uzbekistan. For the President, however, Islam appears important only in its role as a cultural thread running through the new national identity being fostered in the republic. A state-sponsored Islam has become a key part of the regime's attempt to legitimate itself and to shake itself free from its communist past.

In this climate, the number of mosques has increased from 80 at independence to over 5,000 by 1997. The regime has, however, made strenuous efforts to control Islam in Uzbekistan. The central institution for this purpose has been the Moslem Spiritual Department, an organisation originally established by the Bolsheviks as a means to control Islam in Central Asia. The government has also supported state-controlled *madrassas* (theological colleges) as places of moderate Islamic learning. In May 1995, at the behest of the state-controlled Muslim Spiritual Board, President Karimov signed a decree establishing an international Islamic studies centre in Tashkent as a means to develop a distinctly Uzbek form of Islam.

President Karimov has been particularly concerned about the infiltration of unsanctioned Islam from other countries. In August 1997, Karimov recalled some 2,000 Uzbek students studying in Turkey for fear they were being indoctrinated by Islamic clerics. The regime also exercises close control over those who undertake the haj. Surveillance is practised on foreign representatives of Islamic organisations.

Having crushed the secular opposition in the early 1990s, the mosque remains the most important potential focus for political opposition to Karimov and discontent with his failed policies. The Uzbekistani government has launched a range of measures to ensure the compliance of the Islamic clergy. Muslim clerics who deviate from the official endorsed 'moderate' Islam have been arrested or removed from their positions. Mufti Muhammad Yusuf was forced to resign his position as official head of Central Asia's Islamic community in 1993. Yusuf had become the mufti following demonstrations in February 1989 against the Soviet era clerical elite in Uzbekistan. The appointment of Yusuf had marked a liberalisation of Islam in Uzbekistan. Later Yusuf had to leave Uzbekistan to avoid charges of embezzlement and of helping Tajikistan's Islamic movement during the civil war. The drive against independent clerics became particularly intense when Kabul fell to the Taliban in 1996.

The government has been especially active to prevent the development of Islamic political organisations and there is no established Islamic party in Uzbekistan. The Islamic Rebirth Party of Uzbekistan, founded in January 1991, has been inactive since the party chairman, Abdulla quori Otaev, disappeared in December 1992. *Adolat* (Justice), an Islamic group created in 1991, has been banned since March 1992 and its leaders arrested. Under the new law on political parties passed in January 1997, it is illegal to found a party on religious principles. The Committee for Religious Affairs (a Soviet era institution) attached to the Cabinet of Ministers exercises close control over religious institutions in the Republic, particularly in the field of contacts with foreign Islamic organisations.

From 1993 these measures together have generally succeeded in allowing the Uzbekistani authorities to re-establish control over the Islamic clergy. Plans by Islamic groups and leaders to create independent structures have largely been laid aside, while most Islamic community functions, including Islamic education, have reverted to the government's control. The government policy towards Islam has, however, faced problems. On 27th June 1997 Mukhtorjon Khoja Abdullayev, Yusuf's replacement as mufti of Uzbekistan, was removed from his post. It is widely believed that allegations of corruption lay behind his dismissal. In turn he was replaced by Abdurashid Qori Bakhromov, a Karimov loyalist.

On 1 May 1998, the national parliament revised the 1991 law on 'freedom of conscience and religious organisations' imposing new restrictions on religious groups. The law requires that all mosques and religious groups with more than 100 members are registered. The construction of mosques, the establishment of religious associations, and the teaching of theology also require official permission. Theology classes may not be taught in primary and secondary schools and will, instead, be limited to theology colleges. The law also forbids the wearing of religious clothing in public.

While more mainstream or established Islam has been placed firmly under the government's control, a variety of groups have sought to operate independently of the state. The actions of such organisations has been particularly unwelcome by the Karimov regime and since 1992 the government has clamped down on 'unofficial' and political Islam. In recent years the Uzbekistani authorities have identified the Wahhabi movement as a major threat to stability in the country and in Central Asia more generally. The Wahhabis are usually understood as an orthodox group of Sunnis that is dominant in Saudi Arabia, but the term was used in the Soviet era as a short-hand for Islamic fundamentalist. President Karimov has argued that radical Islam is poised to penetrate Central Asia and that Wahhabi proselytism from Saudi Arabia is the central threat, together with the Taliban and the United Opposition in Tajikistan.

Particularly close supervision has been exercised over Islam in the Fergana Valley, the traditional centre for Islam in Central Asia. In this region the Wahhabi insistence on the total adherence to their interpretation of the Koran has earned the movement the label 'fundamentalist'. Islamic leaders and activists from Namangan have been jailed on various charges. Andizhan's main Jami Mosque, built before the 1917 Bolshevik revolution, was closed in 1995 after its chief cleric, Abdu Alil Mirzaev, allegedly the leader of a Wahhabi sect, fell foul of the government and disappeared on the way to Moscow. Mirzaev advocated the organisation of Islamic education and community life free from the government's control.

On 3 December 1997 in Namangan, a group of masked men killed a highly placed official of the transport police (GAI), decapitated him and hung his head in a bag outside the flat of another police official. Attached to the bag was a note reading 'you are next!' Namangan is the historical centre of Islam in Central Asia and the Uzbekistani authorities have been particularly active against Islamic movements in the area. Tashkent responded to the murder by despatching elite troops to the area. On 17 December a suspect, Sohib Kholmatov, apparently a Wahhabi, was located and a gunfight broke out in which three members of the security services were killed, along with Kholmatov.

Following the gun battle, more Islamic radicals were arrested. Reportedly, many were beaten in custody. While cracking down on perceived Wahhabi militants, the authorities rounded up non-Wahhabi Islamic activists and broke up meetings of veiled women. The events around Namangan were not reported in the state media. In fact, despite the government's assertion that Muslim radicals lay behind the deaths, Namangan lies on a well- known drug route and the murder of the policeman could equally have been tied to the activities of organised crime in the region. Eventually 27 individuals were accused of being Islamic militants. In the summer of 1998 a series of show trials were conducted in which various alleged Wahhabis were found guilty of actions connected to the 'the crimes' in Namangan in December 1997. Twenty-six people received prison terms and one was sentenced to death.

The events in Namangan provided the pretext for a sustained assault upon unofficial Islamic groups in Uzbekistan. On the 5th of March 1998, Uzbek security forces surrounded the house of Obidkhan Nazarov, the former Iman of Tashkent's Tokhtabal mosque, in an effort to arrest him and another imam, Yoldash Ergashev, on allegations of interference in state affairs. The two imams were accused of promoting Wahhabism with the goal of overthrowing the government.[19]

On 1 May 1998, while attending the parliamentary session that passed the new law on freedom of conscience, President Karimov spoke out harshly against the Wahhabis, whom he accused of seeking to turn Uzbekistan into a second Tajikistan. Karimov stated that 'such people must be shot in the head. If necessary, I'll shoot them myself, if you lack the resolve.'[20] Later in the same month, while on his first official visit to Russia, Karimov identified joint efforts to combat the spread of fundamentalism in Central Asia as central to future co-operation between the two countries.[21] In an interview published in *Xalq Sozi* on 3 February 1999 President Islam Karimov said that members of the Islamic group called *Hezbi Tahriri Islomiya* are active in the country and represent a threat to security. Karimov said that the group intends to eliminate all administrative boundaries between Islamic countries and form an 'Islamic Caliphate'.[22]

Thus, Islam in Uzbekistan is controlled by a Soviet era organisation the Muftiate or Spiritual Directorate, which strives to confine religion to a peripheral role in society and bans it from any kind of political role. At the same time, the coercive apparatus of the state is engaged against all those who will not conform to officially sanctioned forms of Islamic organisation and activity. What the government most fears is a dissenting tradition as in the Fergana Valley in the south-east, where Muslim leaders have chosen not to become civil servants.

While Islamic groups do not appear to form a coherent network or movement, Islam has emerged as a vehicle for a large number of political and ideological concerns. The emergence of a more organised Islamic opposition may just be a question of time, particularly since the regime's measures against Islamic activists are in danger of becoming counterproductive. Some writers have suggested that secular political opposition may have expired in Uzbekistan. Mirsaidov's apparent retirement from political activity in March 1998, and the dispersal of other opposition figures throughout Europe and the USA, may open the door wider to religious opposition.[23]

On a visit to Tashkent on 20 April 1998, the chairmen of the OSCE, Polish Foreign Minister Bronislav Geremek, warned Karimov that government moves against Islamic groups were likely to be counterproductive. The warning appeared to have little impact on government policy when fifteen men from the eastern city of Andizhan were put on trial in October 1998 on charges of terrorism, possession of arms and drugs, robbery, and extortion. The individuals were identified as Wahhabis. A further five men went on trial the same day in the capital.

The five were also reported to be Wahhabis and to have links to Obidkhan Nazarov, the former Imam of Tashkent's Tokhtoboy Mosque who has been in hiding for nearly one year.[24] On 8 January 1999 a Tashkent court found the five men guilty of trying to overthrow the government and sentenced them to jail terms ranging from two to 12 years.[25]

On 16 February 1999, a series of bomb blasts hit Tashkent, killing 16 and leaving over 130 injured. The bomb attack may have constituted an assassination attempt on President Karimov. In response, the Uzbekistani authorities launched a crackdown in the country, arresting hundreds of people, who were accused of being radical Islamists who underwent training abroad. Speaking at a news conference of the 23 February, Karimov announced 'I can tell you that practically all of the detained persons went through training in Chechnya, Afghanistan, and Tajikistan,' most were Uzbek nationals, he added. Karimov blamed 'religious fanatics' for the blasts and linked the attack to Islamic groups such as Hizbollah, which has waged a violent struggle against Israel, and 'Wahabbis'. He said ethnic Tajik citizens of Uzbekistan were currently undergoing similar training in neighbouring Tajikistan.

As the crackdown expanded, members and supporters of banned political opposition parties and movements, together with their families, were also detained. Islamic radicalism was then linked to secular opposition groups, such as Erk, by the action of the Uzbekistan authorities.

Despite the extensive organisational and coercive actions of the Uzbekistani authorities against Islam, there are therefore strong signs that religion is emerging as a growing source of political opposition in the country. The well-organised and co-ordinated nature of the attacks in Tashkent may suggest, however, that dissatisfied elements within the government or some of the leading figures dismissed by Karimov may lie behind the terror campaign. Whoever is responsible, the carefully nurtured image of Uzbekistan as an island of stability in Central Asia is increasingly being questioned by such developments.

CONCLUSION

Since independence Uzbekistan has emerged as one of the most authoritarian of the post-Soviet republics. The establishment of the new regime has been focused upon the person of President Karimov, the former first Secretary of the Communist Party of Uzbekistan. Karimov has used independence to consolidate a highly personalised form of rule in which all potential competitors for the position of supreme power are removed or demoted. Further, any group or movement that threatens to destabilise the iron grip that the Karimov regime has developed over Uzbekistani society is broken up or ruthlessly suppressed.

The mechanisms by which the Uzbekistani elite has consolidated its control over the Republic are diverse. While coercion and the use of internal security forces has provided an important element of the regime's hold over society, a range of other political mechanisms and ideas have been developed to ensure Karimov's position. Critically, the promotion of Uzbek nationalism and the ability to fuse the former leadership of Soviet Uzbekistan with a specifically national historic narrative has provided a powerful stimulus to mobilise Uzbekistani society beyond the deployment of fear and violence. The regime has also sought to maintain as much of the Soviet era social security system as possible. The provision of a limited safety net has served to continue elements of the welfare authoritarianism characteristic of the Brezhnev era, whereby popular support was bought in return for a protected existence.

With the consolidation of his position in the mid-1990s, Karimov appeared prepared to promote a limited pluralism, in part designed to stem the outflow of Slav and Uzbek professionals. Despite the change in the official tone, no fundamental alterations were made to the policies of the regime. Karimov initially delayed liberalisation because of his desire to limit change to the creation of a 'constructive' opposition (controllable non-governmental organisations), and a media subordinate to the government's censorship and direction. The limited liberalisation before October 1996 led to increasing attempts to express independent views, which were much more critical than desired. The tentative moves towards liberalisation were also undermined by fears about the rise of Islam and economic discontent.

The consolidation of the Karimov regime since independence marks an important break with the past. In place of the Soviet era arrangements, a new form of authoritarianism has been established in Uzbekistan. With power focused on the republican capital Tashkent, with the President almost unchecked, and with the regime legitimated through Uzbek nationalism, the nature of authoritarian rule in Uzbekistan has changed greatly from the Soviet era reliance on the institutions of the Communist Party, state agencies and security services.

Through policies of repression coupled to an aggressive agenda to promote the Uzbek nation, the Karimov regime has succeeded in establishing a form of stability throughout most of Uzbekistan. Major problems remain, however, many as a direct consequent of the form of rule that has emerged in the country. Political stability has been bought at the price of stifling the economic reform critical to the future of the country (see Chapter 3). Political authoritarianism has also established a form of stability that may be far more fragile than the Uzbek leadership would like to admit.

A number of unresolved issues central to the political future of the country continue to cause concern. Alternative political and economic ideas cannot be expressed in a public forum, choking innovation and denying opportunities to express discontent. Corruption, inefficiency and mismanagement characterise much of the political and administrative system. The stress on Uzbek nationalism, has also caused tension in Uzbekistani society. Sizeable and important minorities within Uzbekistan appear uncomfortable with the role of the state in promoting the Uzbek nation over all other groups. The presence of large numbers of ethnic Uzbeks in neighbouring states also makes the pursuit of domestic nationalism a dangerous policy (see Chapter 4).

Regional conflict within Uzbekistan remains significant. Despite the stress on the single Uzbek nation, Uzbek identity is far from consolidated, with areas such as the Fergana Valley causing concern within Tashkent. Political Islam, in particular, remains a force that could emerge to challenge the Karimov regime. The Uzbekistani government has invested extensive effort and resources in the struggle with unofficial Islamic movements in the country. The deep-seated nature of Islam in Uzbekistani society, the heavy-handed tactics of the government, and the lack of secular political movements to offer an alternative medium to articulate grievances may well serve to enhance political Islam and allow it to challenge the model of stability promoted by the repressive leadership of Karimov.

1 William Fierman, 'Political development in Uzbekistan: democratization?' in Karen Dawisha and Bruce Parrott, eds., *Conflict, cleavage, and change in Central Asia and the Caucasus* (Cambridge: CUP, 1997), p. 378.
2 *RFE/RL Newsline*, vol. 2, no. 46, part 1 (9 March 1998).
3 See http://freedomhouse.org/nil-98/uzbek.pdf.
4 *RFE/RL Newsline*, vol. 1, no. 172, part 1 (4 December 1997).
5 *RFE/RL Newsline*, vol. 1, no. 141, part 1 (17 October 1997).
6 *RFE/RL Newsline*, vol. 2, no. 46, part 1 (9 March 1998).

7 Demian Vaisman, 'Regionalism and Clan Loyalty in the Political Life of Uzbekistan' in Yaacov Ro'i, ed., *Muslim Eurasia: Conflicting Legacies* (Essex: Frank Cass, 1995), pp. 105–22.
8 Michael Thurman, 'Leaders of the Communist Party of Uzbekistan in Historical Retrospect: The "Class of '38"' *Central Asia Monitor*, no. 6 (1995), pp. 19–27 and no. 1 (1996), pp. 19–25.
9 Quoted Thurman, *Ibid.*, no. 1 (1996), p. 21.
10 Morgan Liu, 'The Perils of Nationalism in Independent Uzbekistan', *Turkestan Newsletter*, Volume: 91-1: 99 (25 November 1997).
11 Stephen Hegarty, 'The Rehabilitation of Temur: Reconstructing National History in Contemporary Uzbekistan', *Central Asia Monitor*, no. 1 (1995), pp. 28–35.
12 Hegarty, *Ibid.* (1995), p. 29.
13 Annette Bohr, 'Language policy and ethnic relations in Uzbekistan', in Graham Smith, Vivien Law, Andrew Wilson, Annette Bohr, Edward Allwoth, *Nation-building in the Post-Soviet Borderlands: The Politics of National Identity* (Cambridge: CUP, 1998), pp. 197–223.
14 John Schoeberline-Engel, 'The Prospects for Uzbek National Identity', *Central Asia Monitor*, no. 2 (1996), pp. 12–20.
15 *The World Factbook* (Washington: CIA, 1995), p. 447.
16 Vladimir Mesamed, 'Interethnic Relations in the Republic of Uzbekistan,' *Central Asia Monitor*, no. 6 (1996), pp. 20–26.
17 Rahim M. Masov, *Istoriia topornogo razdeleniia* (Dushanbe, 1991), pp. 10–11.
18 Richard Foltz, 'Uzbekistan's Tajiks: A Case of Repressed Identity?', *Central Asia Monitor*, no. 6 (1996), pp. 17–26.
19 *RFE/RL Newsline*, vol. 2, no. 45, part 1 (6 March 1998).
20 *RFE/RL Newsline*, vol. 2, no. 84, part 1 (4 May 1998).
21 *RFE/RL Newsline*, vol. 2, no. 86, part 1 (6 May 1998).
22 *RFE/RL Newsline*, vol. 3. no. 24, part 1 (4 February 1999).
23 *RFE/RL Newsline*, vol. 2, no. 52, part 1 (17 March 1998).
24 *RFE/RL Newsline*, vol. 2, no. 201, part 1 (16 October 1998).
25 *RFE/RL Newsline*, vol. 3, no. 6, part 1 (11 January 1999).

Chapter 3

ECONOMY AND SOCIETY

INTRODUCTION

The nature and intensity of economic activity in Uzbekistan has undergone important developments in the twentieth century; however, despite such change the basic structure of the economy remains in essence the same as it has for centuries. Today, the vast majority of the labour force is engaged in agriculture and this remains the core sector of the national economy. Under Russian and Soviet rule, cotton became the dominant agricultural product in the region and in the 1990s the cotton crop continues to provide the foundation for the whole economy of Uzbekistan.

Following the collapse of the Soviet state in the summer of 1991, Uzbekistan faced severe problems associated with the demise of the all-union economy, which had underpinned the Soviet system. The collapse of the trade and supplier networks of the Soviet economy left Uzbekistan particularly exposed. With little other than raw or semi-processed commodities for export, the economic system in the country became highly dependent upon world commodity prices. Creating an economic system to minimise the vulnerability of the economy to external shocks would have required extensive reform and the introduction of market-based elements. Instead, President Karimov developed a set of policies oriented primarily towards extending control over the economy rather than implementing structural reforms.

Since 1991, the Uzbekistani state has retained and even enhanced its previous position as the pivot of the national economy. Much of the social welfare system of the Soviet period has continued, even as the state's ability to support such a system has declined. Economic reform has been limited and frequently ineffective. Foreign investment has been low, and the government of Uzbekistan has been reluctant to undertake the reform measures advocated by the IMF, the World Bank and other international economic institutions. Corruption, inefficiency and bureaucratic resistance frequently stifle efforts to develop new business initiatives.

In an environment of extensive state control, the Uzbekistani economy has struggled to make progress. Despite optimistic official economic data, most independent commentators point to stagnation or negative growth as the main characteristic of the national economy. The distorted sectoral structure of the national economy together with the lack of significant reform, widespread corruption, increasing demographic pressures and the ecological crisis are placing an intense strain upon the already largely bankrupt Soviet-era economy. If Uzbekistan is to become the developed country that the authorities have repeatedly promised, fundamental and systematic reform of the economy will be urgently required in future years.

HISTORICAL ECONOMIC FORMS AND THE SILK ROAD

Central Asia's geographical position ensured that as early as the sixth century BC the region was engaged in significant trade with external markets. Traditionally, the main elements of Central Asian exports were horses, handicrafts, textiles and dried fruits. Reflecting the significance of the Central Asian trade routes, the region remained economically important even as the Silk Road was being challenged by the development of global maritime trade in the sixteenth century. Despite the emergence of new trading routes, and the rise of advanced forms of agriculture and industrial activity in Europe, Central Asia continued to be an important economic region until the eighteenth century. As the region entered a period of comparative decline, trade links with India, Iran, and western China remained important.

The early emergence of Central Asia as a centre for economic activity owed much to the favourable conditions in the area. Central Asia's important water resources and good soils made the region an excellent location for the production of agricultural goods. The mix of extensive plains, oases, and deep mountain valleys also created the basis for the production of a variety of agriculture products. The abundance of foodstuffs provided a critical foundation for the emergence of large urban areas, which developed around the main oases of the region.

The region was not only able to provide sufficient resources to feed its own population but also supplied agricultural products, notably natural fibres and animals, for export. The development of small-scale agriculture was primarily a private activity and until the early part of the twentieth century, private ownership was the main organisational form for economic activity. In the settled areas, the individual household provided the basis for the urban economy.

The growth of urban areas laid the foundations for new and more advanced forms of economic activity. The towns developed markets for high quality handicrafts such as carpets and other textiles, often produced in the rural areas and by nomads. The emergence of guild organisations within the settled areas also led to the production of jewellery and a range of household goods.

By the eighteenth century, Central Asia had entered a period of relative economic decline. The emergence of new and advanced forms of economic activity in Europe, particularly Russia, gradually led to the marginalisation of Central Asia. Central Asia entered a period of stagnation with little change in economic forms or levels of economic activity. The regional economy of Central Asia only began to undergo significant change when Central Asia came into contact with the Russian colonial state.

THE RUSSIAN AND SOVIET LEGACY

Russian conquest of Central Asia introduced important changes in many aspects of the region, but the regional economy was initially little affected by absorption into the Russian empire. As the territories and peoples of Central Asia were steadily integrated into the Russian imperial economy, however, important changes were introduced. New types of economic activity were developed, notably the extraction of mineral resources and limited industrial production. Communications between Central Asia, European Russia and world markets were also significantly improved. The greatest change to the economy of the Transoxiana region of Central Asia under Russian domination was, however, in the organisation and intensity of economic activity, particularly in the agricultural sphere.

The Russian colonial regime initiated important shifts in the agricultural orientation of the core region of Central Asia. The changes introduced under Russian administration were to have critical consequences for the future economic development of the area. The particular focus of Russian development in the region was an increase and intensification of cotton production.

When the Russians arrived in Central Asia they found traces of the once complex irrigation systems that existed in the region, but which had been allowed to deteriorate or had been destroyed over previous centuries. Under Russian control many of the canals were rebuilt and the area of irrigated land expanded. The main purpose of increasing the irrigated acreage was to boost the production of cotton and grain and thereby to decrease Russian reliance on sources of supply from outside the empire.

In the early 1880s, the Russian colonial regime introduced new higher yield American varieties of cotton into Turkestan. The total land under American-cotton cultivation increased six-fold from 1886 to 1890. In the period 1886 to 1914 the acreage increased from 13,200 to 597,200 hectares. The boom in cotton production had a number of significant effects. The rise of cotton production was paralleled by the growth in the grain deficit. Central Asia, which had previously been self-sufficient in grain, became increasingly dependent upon grain imported from Russia. The cotton boom also created the basis for a more monetised economy, allowing for the importation of Russian industrial goods. The growth of cotton production was also accompanied by a rise of industrial activity centred upon the production of cotton.

At the time of Russian conquest, local industry was engaged primarily in the processing of cotton, wool and silk, and limited production based upon these fibres. Even in the urban areas of Transoxiana there was little developed modern industry. Production was focused on the manufacture of handicrafts at home or in small workshops. Initially, contact with the Russian empire served to undermine many indigenous industries. With the advent of Russian trade, the small metalworking industry went into decline, replaced by cheaper and higher quality imported goods.

Some new forms of economic activity were, however, introduced. In 1865 the Russian colonial regime undertook a systematic survey of the mineral resources of the region, which provided the basis for the development of extractive industries. The working of coal was undertaken in Uzbekistan but never really grew to be significant, oil deposits were also exploited to a limited degree in the region.

From the point of view of the future economic development of southern Central Asia, one of most important aspects of the Russian colonial period was the establishment of modern transport infrastructure connecting the core of Central Asia to other parts of the Russian Empire, and beyond. The Trans-Caspian Railway reached Samarkand in 1888 and was extended to Tashkent in 1898 and to Andizhan in the Fergana Valley in 1899. In 1906, the Orenburg-Tashkent Railroad was completed. The introduction of American style cotton gins in the 1880s and the extension of the Trans-Caspian railway to the main cotton growing regions of Central Asia provided the basis for important changes in the basis and nature of economic activity in the region. The cotton mills quickly came to employ two-thirds of all industrial workers and accounted for over three-fourths of the total industrial production. Most cotton grown in Central Asia was transported from the region to Russia for processing into textiles.

Despite the changes introduced under Russian rule, no real efforts were made to initiate a broad-based industrialisation of southern Central Asia before 1917. When the Russian Revolution broke out, mining was in its infancy, coal and oil production elementary, and no iron or steel was manufactured in Central Asia. The processing of agricultural products, especially cotton, provided the mainstay of industrial activity in the region.

During the Soviet period there were important changes in agricultural and industrial activity in Uzbekistan. Despite the innovations introduced by the Soviets, however, much of the development undertaken during seventy years of communist rule was simply an extension of Tsarist era policies. Agricultural development in Uzbekistan during the Soviet period was, in particular, largely a projection of pre-1917 Russian policy with the emphasis upon the expansion of cotton production and a decline in grain and other foodstuffs.

Following the consolidation of Soviet rule in the region in the 1920s there were two principal alterations to the nature of agriculture in Uzbekistan. The first major change in the region was the confiscation of lands and water rights, and their redistribution to the peasantry. This was followed by the second policy change, that of collectivisation, through which lands and water were brought under the control of the Party and its rural representatives.

Collectivisation in Uzbekistan was, however, relatively superficial compared to developments in neighbouring Kazakhstan and Kyrgyzstan where collectivisation led to the wholesale destruction of the nomadic economy. In Uzbekistan several elements of traditional forms of land ownership were incorporated into the collective and state farms. In many areas of Uzbekistan, collectivisation permitted the survival of traditional forms of social organisation and political relationships. Nevertheless, together these reforms provided the basis for an unprecedented state-directed expansion of cotton production in Uzbekistan.

The main economic activity in Uzbekistan during the Soviet era was the production of cotton and other agricultural products. Indeed, Uzbekistan was often described as a country that was two-thirds desert and one-third cotton fields. During the civil war, the acreage of irrigated land fell precipitously and farmers switched from cotton production to grain. After the civil war and the *Basmachi* revolt, the first action of the Soviets was to restore the irrigation system. By 1928 irrigated land was approaching the pre-1917 levels and the emphasis on cotton production had returned. The southern part of Central Asia became more firmly tied to the Russian core of the Soviet system as a one-crop region. Uzbekistan set the pattern for the development of cotton production in Central Asia. By 1932 the Uzbeks were raising about 61 percent of all cotton fibre produced in the USSR.

The beginning of the First Five-Year Plan in 1928 saw a further extension of the area under cotton and a gradual decline in other crops. As pre-Revolutionary production levels were restored, the next main upheaval was the collectivisation drive that reached its height in Uzbekistan in 1930–31. Collectivisation led to a fall in cotton production and this prompted the drive to intensify productivity through the increased application of fertiliser.

During World War Two, cotton production declined once again as other priorities emerged. Following the war, the emphasis on cotton returned. Irrigation in the form of new canals was developed and the level of cotton production increased. In the final decades of Soviet control, Central Asia accounted for about 90 percent of total production of cotton in the USSR. The land committed to the production of cotton in Uzbekistan steadily rose from 423.5 thousand hectares in 1913 to 917.2 in 1938 and 2,054.0 thousand hectares in 1986. The legacy of this policy has been a set of chronic ecological problems and a largely rural and unskilled workforce.

Although cotton production dominated the agricultural sector during the Soviet years, Uzbekistan was also the location for an important development in the form of the steady expansion of private plot production. Although officially discouraged, the private plot became an essential element of the Soviet economy as the state-controlled agricultural sector as a whole failed to deliver the required quantities of foodstuffs. In Uzbekistan the role of private plots in agriculture was increasing in the final years of the Soviet Union. By 1978, private plots accounted for 20.9 percent of Uzbek gross output, and the figure may have been as high as 28 percent and over a third of a collective farmer's income.

Unlike the Russian colonial period, the Soviet era in Uzbekistan was marked by a significant conscious attempt to develop industry in the region. During the Civil War the limited industry of the region disintegrated and by 1922 industry had collapsed completely. The period from 1922–1928 was marked by efforts to restore industry and agriculture to pre-1917 levels. Between 1928 and the outbreak of the Second World War the industrialisation of southern Central Asia proceeded more rapidly based in large part on the electrification of the region. The period saw the construction of a large textile mill in Tashkent in 1935. Under the Second Five-Year Plan, industry was particularly stressed and several new enterprises were begun, mostly in the agro-industrial sector.

The onset of war led to important changes in economic activity in Uzbekistan. Of particular note was the emergence of steel production, often using hydroelectric power developed in other republics of Central Asia. The emphasis on industry as the auxiliary to cotton production was continued after the war with the construction of factories to produce agricultural machinery in Tashkent. Oil production was also expanded in Uzbekistan and natural gas deposits were worked around the city of Bukhara.

Transportation was also developed to a far higher level than previously under Soviet rule. The much-vaunted Turkistan-Siberian Railway was completed in 1930. The construction of the line was intended to make possible the delivery of increased grain to southern Central Asia from other parts of the Soviet Union, so freeing more land for cotton production. The development of roads was, however, very poor, reflecting the economic priorities of the planners in Moscow. But important airports were constructed in Uzbekistan during the latter decades of the Soviet system.

A major achievement of the Soviet period was an increase in the human capital of Uzbekistan. With an adult literacy rate of 97.2% in 1989, the education level of the population was high, and vastly improved from the levels of the Russian colonial era. The Soviets established a comprehensive educational system in Uzbekistan including some high quality institutions of higher education. The scientific potential of the country was concentrated in over 350 establishments and well-trained research personnel were engaged in work on a number of areas of basic research. The emigration of some of the most skilled members of society in recent years has, however, damaged the scientific and research base of the country.

Thus, during the Soviet era Uzbekistan's economy underwent a series of fundamental changes, including an extensive re-organisation of agriculture, an intensification of production and the introduction of new industries. Despite the introduction of new economic activity, the pattern of economic expansion in southern Central Asia during the

Soviet period was largely one-sided; focused upon the production of cotton. The socialist system with its planned economy, state-socialist political institutions and economic priorities left the Uzbek economy poorly prepared for independence.

Despite talk of developing self-sufficiency in the region, Uzbekistan was firmly anchored to the rest of the USSR by economic dependency. In the Soviet Union, Uzbekistan functioned primarily as a supplier of raw materials that were processed elsewhere. As a result, official figures placed Uzbekistan as one of the poorer of the republics in the USSR with only Tajikistan having a lower per capita consumption. Despite Uzbekistan's extensive natural resource base (estimated to total $13 trillion), Soviet planners did little to create indigenous industry capable of exploiting these resources.

Three distinct sorts of distortion in the Uzbek economy resulted from the Soviet system. First, the Soviet centrally planned economy failed to establish the institutions necessary to ensure stability once the planner's control was relaxed. During the Soviet years, the Uzbek economy was largely run from Moscow, ensuring that poor local administration characterised much of the republican economy. Critically, there was an absence of indigenous financial instruments for economic management. Uzbekistan lacked a developed banking system, a capital or money market, an effective fiscal system in the form of a tax regime and the instruments necessary for the formulation and implementation of effective macro-economic policy. As elsewhere in the former Soviet Union, the planned economy meant that production was not very efficiently organised and there was no effective price system to regulate demand and supply.

Second, despite improvements in transport links the non-human infrastructure of the country was poorly developed during the Soviet years. While the railway and road networks were built to connect Uzbekistan to the Russian Federation and other republics of the former Soviet Union, most routes leading out of Uzbekistan to the south, west and east were weakly developed and needed to be upgraded if trade and transit were to increase. The communication links from Uzbekistan across Central Asia were particularly poor. The telecommunications system was extremely underdeveloped with only 7/8 telephones per 100 population and the quality of transmission was generally very low.

Third, the incorporation and development of Uzbekistan within the planned economy resulted in the development of highly distorted economic structures. Agricultural and industrial capacity was developed with very little regard to the needs of republic's population. Such economic development produced an excessive trade dependency. Productivity was low and the economy's ability to satisfy consumer's expectations even lower. The Soviet model of economic development ensured that the service sector remained almost completely underdeveloped.

Together this set of distortions also had important implications for the emergence of networks of corruption within Uzbekistan. The concentration of economic and political decision-making within the party-state apparatus and the dependence of the local elite on the production of cotton meant that a powerful patrimonial system developed around the agro-industrial sector in the republic. The long tenure of Rashidov as first secretary in the UzSSR during the Brezhnev period enabled the creation of a personal fiefdom, with the appointment of his followers to senior posts in the republican, *oblast* and local levels. Despite the extensive assault on corrupt practices in Uzbekistan during the 1980s, at independence the political economy of the republic remained heavily informed by the culture and practices that developed in the Soviet years.[1]

INDEPENDENCE AND REFORM

Since independence, the main characteristic of economic policy in Uzbekistan has been a high degree of government direction, intended officially to provide a cushion for the social dislocation brought about by the introduction of market-oriented reforms. In fact, more often, this policy agenda has been a thinly veiled disguise for the preservation of autocratic political control and the continuation (and often expansion) of state-based corruption.

At the official level, the Uzbek model of economic development has been identified as consisting of five major principles. First, the economy has supposedly been given priority over politics, and thus there has been a de-ideologisation of external and domestic economic relations. Second, the state is identified as the main source of reform. Third, the preservation of law and order and the supremacy of the law are given a strong emphasis. Fourth, the Uzbek model stresses the provision of an extensive system of social protection for the population from the harsh consequences of economic reform. Finally, an evolutionary transition to a free market is envisaged. In fact, with the possible exceptions of the preservation of social policies from the Soviet era and the leading role of the state, the Uzbek economy rarely approaches any of the elements identified as the stated aims of economic development.

The government's gradualist approach to economic and structural reform in Uzbekistan did little to raise the performance of the national economy in the first years of independence. The World Bank estimates that there was a fall in real GDP of 15% between 1992 and 1994. The sectors most affected were construction and industry, which faced severe problems in receiving necessary supplies from other states of the former Soviet Union (FSU). Although these figures are high, they fall below the average output decline in the rest of the FSU.

In the early years of independence, a major challenge facing Uzbekistan was rising inflation. After 1991, hyperinflation quickly took hold of the Uzbekistani economy. In 1992 inflation reached 520% and in 1993 1,100%. Uzbekistan left the Moscow dominated rouble zone in November 1993 and introduced its own transitional national currency, the Som-coupon. In July 1994 the new national currency (the Som) was introduced. IMF data suggests that in the early years of independence there was little progress in bringing inflation under control. Inflation at the end of 1994 stood at 1,232.8%. Following the introduction of the Som, however, the government gradually raised the official exchange rate so that it was close to the black market rate. Slowly inflation was brought under control such that by the spring of 1998 the monthly inflation figure stood at about 2.4% (giving an annual level of 32.9%).

With the Uzbekistani economy making slow progress in the early years of independence, in 1994 President Karimov sought to accelerate the reform process. On 21 January the President issued a major decree 'On Measures for Further Deepening Economic Reforms, Providing for the Protection of Private Property and for the Development of Entrepreneurship'. Seen at the time as a turning point for economic reform in the country, the decree bolstered the power of the state to promote economic reform. An inter-ministerial committee on economic reform, entrepreneurship and foreign investment was established, there was an expansion of the powers of the privatisation committee to include aspects of private sector development. In addition, stock, housing and commodity exchanges were planned, permission for persons to hold foreign currency accounts was granted, import duties were eliminated for one year and a state insurance company capable of guaranteeing foreign investments was established.

The introduction in 1994 of a comprehensive reform programme, which was supported by the President, had important consequences for the Uzbekistani economy. By the end of 1995 inflation fell to around 10% per month. The small amount of data available suggests that during this period the government was maintaining a restrictive monetary policy in accordance with the IMF demands. The Central Bank cut interest rates as inflation fell, but ensured that rates remained positive in real terms. Official figures released at the beginning of 1996 suggested that GDP declined by just 1% in 1995, with real industrial output rising by 0.2%.

The nature and pace of reform, however, was criticised by the IMF. Despite the changes of 1994, it was only in 1995 that anything approaching a coherent stabilisation package began to appear in Uzbekistan. A particular point of criticism was the mixed performance of structural reform. The IMF was worried by Uzbekistan's failure to restructure enterprises and the way in which privatisation was conducted.

One area that the IMF identified for praise in Uzbekistan was the withdrawal of state subsidies. In response to Russia's decision to introduce price liberalisation on 2 January 1992, prices for basic foodstuffs in Uzbekistan were capped and subsidies to certain sectors were doubled in an effort to soften the blow. The World Bank estimated that consumer subsidy and enterprise credits amounted to at least 21% of GDP in 1993. By the middle of 1994, however, many of the subsidies that had existed for food, utilities, housing, transport and energy had been removed.

While supporting price liberalisation, the IMF was critical of the way that economic policy was developed. In particular, the IMF questioned the independence of the Central Bank and called on the President to reduce 'administrative interventions' in the economy. Nevertheless, by the end of 1995 the Uzbek economy appeared to be making progress and foreign investors grew more optimistic about the prospects for economic development. In 1996, however, many of the problems that the IMF and other international organisations had identified within the Uzbek economy became acute causing major economic problems.

In 1995 the disastrous domestic cotton harvest and low world prices for the commodity led the Uzbek leadership to impose foreign exchange controls and to begin to print money, thereby stoking up inflation once again. The heavy-handed actions of the government led the IMF to suspend a $185 million standby loan on 19 December 1996 on the grounds that Uzbekistan had missed its inflation targets. The imposition of tight state controls over currency transactions caused severe problems for foreign firms operating in Uzbekistan and foreign investment slowed to a trickle.

The problems associated with the crisis in state finances effectively spelled the end of the limited economic reforms that had hitherto been introduced in Uzbekistan. A strong critic of the more radical economic transitions attempted among the other ex-Soviet republics, President Karimov justified freezing market reforms in late 1996 for fear of sparking unrest among the population. During 1997 and 1998 the Uzbek government failed to launch significant economic change in the country as political issues and control over Uzbek society increasingly became the central focus of the ruling elite.

The government remained resistant to pressure to restructure and privatise enterprises and postponed privatisation in the oil and gas sectors. By 1998, the government remained reluctant to conclude an agreement on a standby loan facility with the IMF in the face of conditions requiring a move towards currency convertibility. The European Bank for Reconstruction and Development and the US Commerce Department criticised the government for creating a difficult business environment.

Equally, there was little indication that the government would launch the critical structural reforms urgently needed by the economy. The state continued to dominate all sectors of the economy through a range of direct and indirect methods. The poor quality and deliberate official distortion of state statistics suggests that many of the government's claims regarding apparent successes in reducing inflation and improving trade may be exaggerated. The country remains perilously dependent upon the sale of cotton to world markets at advantageous prices. The problems of the Uzbek economy are concentrated in six particular areas:

ECONOMIC INSTITUTIONS

A central problem for Uzbekistan has been the lack of the developed institutional infrastructure necessary for the management and successful operation of a market economy. In response to the new demands of macro and micro-economic management, some efforts were initially undertaken to create appropriate new structures. Given the strong culture of state intervention in the economy, high levels of corruption and personalised rule, as well as the, at best, semi-marketised nature of the Uzbekistani economy, establishing new institutional arrangements has proved particularly difficult. Personal networks, contacts and families ties have come to substitute for independent and strong institutions.

Although Uzbekistan supports an elaborate structure of economics and finance ministries, the President and his Council are the locus for all major economic decisions. Uzbekistan's economic priorities are set out in a series of books and speeches produced by President Karimov, although usually written by his advisors and researchers, such as *Don't' Knock Down The Old House Before You Have Built The New One*, *Along The Road Of Deepening Reform*, *Uzbekistan On The Threshold Of The Twenty-first Century*. The Ministry of finance develops the state budget, exercises financial supervision of enterprises and manages all inter-governmental credit agreements and international financial institutions and oversees foreign currency loans to enterprises. The Ministry oversees external debt servicing and manages re-payments.

The Central Bank is supposedly subordinated only to parliament. In fact, it is the government that in practice controls the Bank. The ability of the Central Bank to make independent decisions has been frequently called into question, as has its ability to control the banking sector in the country. In 1994, a banking reform was launched. A two-tier system was established consisting of the Central Bank and about 30 commercial banks. The main aim of the reform was to restrict the availability of credit to enterprises, a major source of inflation. The poor supervision of the commercial sector by the Central Bank has frequently undermined this aim and the continuing access to cheap credit has weakened the process of enterprise privatisation.

The failure to foster independent economic institutions has ensured that all aspects of the economy remain subordinated to the priorities and directives of the President. This environment has prevented the emergence of autonomous centres for economic decision-making and the creation of mechanisms for investment driven by economic efficiency. Instead, even the commercial banking sector has been tied to the state system and banks allocate credit to priority sectors as identified by the government.

The lack of autonomous economic institutions means that while Uzbekistan has important visible elements of a market economy (the large markets for foodstuffs in each town for example) it is impossible to talk of a significant market-based private sector in Uzbekistan. All economic activity remains hinged upon the Uzbek state and key figures in the ruling elite. Government control of the local judges and courts means that there is little or no protection from state intrusion into economic activity. Even the policies of privatisation have failed to foster the establishment of the autonomous business organisations at the heart of market economies.

PRIVATISATION

Initially, the government of Uzbekistan appeared to be pursuing the development of the private sector in Uzbekistan through policies of privatisation. The government adopted a gradual privatisation with the law 'On Denationalisation and Privatisation' passed in November 1991 providing the basis for the process. To support the privatisation drive, the Committee for the Management of State Property (GKI) was established in February 1992. In stage one of privatisation, the GKI undertook the disposal of housing, agriculture and the retail sector. In 1994–95, stage two of the privatisation process was begun with over 5,000 enterprises to be privatised.

The pace of privatisation accelerated in March 1994 with the decree 'On Top Priority Directions for Further Development of Denationalisation and Privatisation'. At the same time, President Karimov announced that the state would no longer finance insolvent enterprises. By the end of 1994, the GKI estimated there to be 67,660 enterprises in Uzbekistan of which 20,758 were state enterprises and 46,902 private or privatised. In February 1995, President Karimov claimed that privatisation had been very successful and that 100,000 firms, or 67% of state firms, and most of the workforce were in the private sector. Privatisation, however, has only enjoyed very limited success with various enterprises still under the influence of central or local government to significant degrees.

Since the mid-1990s the privatisation programme has slowed considerably. In 1998 the government planned to privatise 346 state-owned firms. But in many cases the state retained a sizeable or controlling stake. In May 1998 the government announced that the privatisation of the oil and gas sectors was being postponed. Given the slow rate of privatisation, many insolvent firms have continued to function supported by the state. However, even where privatisation has been carried out the results are often far from favourable for the new owners.

Critically, the state has retained strategic stakes in most enterprises. State control over credit facilities, exchange controls, price formation and the activities of various bureaucratic agencies (principally the tax inspectorate) has ensured that even nominally private enterprises operate in a tightly state-defined framework. Shareholders have no influence over firms. Privatisation has been heavily influenced by contacts to the government and has frequently served as the basis for the construction of networks of political patronage. Associates of the government and their families staff the most profitable firms. Monopolies are unregulated and serve as the basis for rent seeking rather than raising production or efficiency.

FINANCES

In 1992, Uzbekistan ran a fiscal debt of 11% of GDP. In 1993 the debt fell to 9% and in 1993 to 4.8%. In the early years of independence the government had problems controlling spending because credit was made available to enterprises and the government sought to maintain public expenditure in the social and cultural sectors. As Uzbekistan began to abide by the IMF conditions, government spending appeared to be brought under control. In May 1996 it was announced that Uzbekistan had posted a deficit-free budget for the first quarter of the year. Initially, Uzbekistan's external debt remained small relatively, as it did not inherit the debt of the former Soviet Union, which became the responsibility of the Russian Federation at independence. In mid-1994, the total external debt stood at about $700m. The economic crisis that afflicted the economy from 1996 onwards has, however, placed severe strain on the debt situation in Uzbekistan.

Facing difficulties raising external credit because of the failure to conclude an agreement with the IMF, the Uzbek authorities have sought to keep the fiscal accounts close to balance by running up wage and pension arrears, forcing loans from local banks, and retaining a tight grip on local enterprises and their exports. The Economist Intelligence Unit (EIU) estimates that the consolidated fiscal deficit in the country is running at about 3%, but with wage arrears and unpaid taxes the deficit is considerably higher.[2]

Given the poor state of government finances, the trade situation has become critical. In the early years of independence Uzbekistan did not appear to experience a major deterioration in its balance of trade and in 1994 a small trade surplus was posted. According to the Ministry of Foreign Economic Relations, the 1995 trade balance was in surplus to the tune of $293 million, with exports at $1.89bn and imports at $1.6bn. The heavy reliance on cotton exports, however, has meant that Uzbekistan's trade balance is at the mercy of the world cotton markets.

The poor cotton harvest and fall in world prices for cotton in 1995–96 caused severe problems in balancing trade flows. Data for the first months of 1998 point to falling levels of exports and imports, although trade data are generally scarce. The fall in world prices for ferrous and non-ferrous metals has also hit exports. The EIU predicts a trade deficit in 1998 of $130 million rising to $220 in 1999.[3] The trade deficit is, however, managed by a steadily depreciating national currency, which prices imports out of the local market.

Given the problems with government finances, lack of international credit and poor trade figures, the Uzbek government is running a significant current account deficit. The EIU has predicted a worsening of the current account deficit to around $280 million in 1998 and 1999.[4] Although the current account deficit is significant, it is anticipated that it will remain manageable as long as there is no collapse in exports, particularly cotton exports.

AGRICULTURE

Agriculture forms the backbone of the Uzbekistani economy and although the country consists of over 60% arid or semi-arid steppe, Uzbekistan also has a number of highly fertile regions. Due to the significance of agriculture, developing the sector effectively will be a key component to reform of the Uzbek economy. In 1994, agriculture accounted for 44% of GDP. The single most important crop in Uzbekistan is cotton. Uzbekistan is the fourth largest producer of seed cotton and the second largest exporter of cotton in the world. It is also the largest producer of silk and karakul pelts in the FSU. Other important products include wheat, rice, tobacco and fruits, and vegetables. Despite the large share of agriculture in the economy, Uzbekistan is not self-sufficient. A large portion of foodstuffs are imported, including wheat 66%, meat 30%, milk 25%, and potatoes 50%.

The form of agriculture inherited from the Soviet era, with its reliance on the extensive use of land, water and chemicals (fertilisers and pesticides) has been particularly damaging to the environment. Uzbekistan has a large but inefficient irrigation system to provide water for cotton production, and it is this system that has lain at the heart of the problems of the Aral Sea and the over use of water supplies. Irrigating the cotton monoculture has overstretched water resources in the region leading to the desiccation of the Aral Sea, which has shrunk from the world's fourth largest inland lake to the ninth largest and now has only a quarter of its 1960 volume. It is predicted that the lake will disappear entirely early in the next century. The saline dust, industrial wastes, pesticides and fertilisers that have poisoned the remaining subsurface and surface waters, land and air in the region, compound the environmental problems associated with cotton production.

In an attempt to decrease environmental pollution, ameliorate the problems around the Aral Sea, a policy of shifting agriculture production to grain has been introduced. The shift to grain production was also intended to change Uzbekistan's dependence on the importation of foodstuffs and help redress the balance of payments problem. The 1995-grain harvest was put by the authorities at 2.7m tons, an improvement on the 1994 harvest but still well below the official target of 3.3m tons. Since 1990, the area sown for grain has increased from 1.010m ha to 1.529m ha.

Despite the poor initial harvests, President Karimov persisted with the view that Uzbekistan should be self-sufficient in food. As a result, the area given over to grain is forecast to rise further. In 1998, the outlook for grain production was better than at anytime since the policy of cereal self-sufficiency was launched in 1995. Up to 1.6m ha have been devoted to grain production. The 1998 harvest may be as high as 3.6m tonnes for wheat and 100,000 tonnes of barley.

Cotton production continues to be of critical importance to Uzbekistan. The area devoted to cotton remains constant at 1.5m ha. Cotton production has now fallen steadily since reaching a high of 5.365m tons in 1988. Since 1995, the cotton crop has consistently fallen below target, causing severe problems for the whole economy. Although recent years have seen a rise in the cotton harvest from the disastrous yields of 1995–96, most regions have failed to reach their production targets. In 1998, the cotton harvest was again below the plan, this time by up to 12%.[5] The worst hit region has been Karakalpakstan, which has suffered from dwindling water resources. Although the Uzbek strategy is to decrease steadily cotton production, the fortunes of the whole economy will continue to hinge upon the cotton harvest for some years. Raising the quality and productivity of the cotton crop would greatly assist the prospects of successfully restructuring the rest of the economy.

One of the most important changes for agriculture has been the abolition of state farms and their conversion to co-operative enterprises. Members of the new collectives do not have the right to sell their shares. Some private farms have developed. In 1994 there were 10,408, and there have been plans for a significant expansion of the numbers of private farms. Often the end of the collective farm structure has made little difference to the management of agriculture land since the former networks of power retain a tenacious grip on the rural population.

The percentage of land available for private farming by the farm workers has risen significantly (110,000 ha before 1991 to 630,000 ha in 1994). Land itself is not privatised, although agricultural land can be traded within the *Mahalla*, and land attached to an enterprise can be sold with that enterprise. In a speech on 24 December 1997 President Karimov ruled out the complete privatisation of land, arguing that the cotton sector could not operate using private land. A principal problem of the agricultural sector in Uzbekistan has been the failure to modernise the food processing industry to produce better quality goods and provide safe and convenient packaging.

MINING, ENERGY AND INDUSTRY

Uzbekistan has extensive mineral reserves. The development of mining and the processing of minerals and metals have been identified as major priorities by the government. Uzbekistan has 30 gold deposits and ranks eighth in the world in terms of gold processing. Close to 70 tons of gold are extracted annually. There are also important deposits of other important non-ferrous metals, including copper, lead, zinc, tungsten and lithium.

Metals production in Uzbekistan has risen steadily in recent years, particularly in the gold sector. The Newport-Zarafshan joint venture has reversed the slide in gold production. Other metals such as copper, silver and non-ferrous metals are also being produced in increasing amounts. The export of metals has emerged as a critical element of Uzbek trade with the rest of the world, second only to cotton production.

Uzbekistan also has important reserves of hydrocarbons and the government has pursued a policy of becoming self-sufficient in fuel with some success. There have been no significant imports of oil since

1994 and none since 1995. The refining industry has also performed well, raising production steadily over recent years. Oil production has risen but now appears to be levelling off. Domestic oil prices remain low reflecting the government's policy of subsidising the domestic economy.

Uzbekistan ranks 10th in the world in terms of gas extraction. Gas production has also risen in recent years, although not at the same pace as the increase in oil output. In 1994, about 48bn cubic meters of gas were produced. By 1997 production had reached 51.2bn cu metres. If gas is to be exported in serious volumes, however, investment in a modern infrastructure including gas pipelines and refineries will be required. Uzbekistan has also faced serious difficulties in obtaining payment for the gas exported to neighbouring states (4.9bn cubic metres in 1996). In recent years, supplies to Tajikistan, Kazakhstan and Kyrgyzstan have been reduced or cut off due to none payment.

The oil and gas sector has been very attractive to foreign investors, and France and Japan have agreed to provide $200m to finance the modernisation of the Bukhara refinery, which is being undertaken by Technip of France. Unlike Kazakhstan, Uzbekistan does not plan to become a major exporter of oil but rather achieve self-sufficiency. Foreign investment is to finance the development of the Mingbulak and Kokdumalak fields as a way to lift total output. By 2000–2010 it is planned that annual production will reach 9m tons.

Industry in Uzbekistan is largely confined to light industry. Despite the importance of cotton and silk production, only a small percentage of the fibres are processed domestically. Uzbekistan relies heavily on textile imports. The development of an indigenous textile industry has been given high priority. The importance of the agricultural sector is reflected in the fact that a significant part of industrial activity is concerned with agro-industrial production; agricultural machinery and fertilisers.

An important new departure for the domestic economy is the production of small trucks and cars, and diesel engine buses. A number of foreign firms have established production facilities in Uzbekistan and the country is set to become a regional centre for the automotive sector. In 1995, Daimler-Benz expanded vehicle production in Uzbekistan and in March 1996, Daewoo opened a plant in Tashkent, which will eventually produce 30,000 cars and vans annually.

Tourism has considerable potential because of the country's unique historical sites. The lack of an adequate infrastructure of transport, hotels and recreation facilities, however, means that the potential of tourism has yet to be fulfilled. Like almost all sectors of the Uzbek economy, the success of tourism will be dependent on foreign involvement. The poor general climate for investment in the country has, however, discouraged extensive developments in the tourist industry.

INTERNATIONAL FINANCE AND INVESTMENT

External capital, whether private or public, could play a decisive role in the economic fortunes of Uzbekistan. A number of western firms have made sizeable investments in Uzbekistan. Daewoo has invested nearly $450 million in its car factories, while British American Tobacco has begun the production of cigarettes at a number of sites and plans the construction of new manufacturing facilities. Other important western firms are active in the mining, energy and telecommunications sectors.

The activity of foreign firms has been underpinned by financial assistance and guarantees provided by foreign governments. In April 1995, the Uzbekistan government received credit from the Export-Import Bank of Japan for the development of Kokdumalak oil and gas field, while in June 1995 Germany provided DM 240m for the renovation of Tashkent airport. A range of other large projects has received backing from the international financial community.

Large international organisations have provided the final layer of assistance for market reforms and investment, offering finance for individual sectors of the economy and also for macro-economic projects. The World Bank initially extended credit worth $160 million to establish a stabilisation fund for the Uzbekistani national currency and the Economic Bank for Reconstruction and Development (EBRD) has provided finance to develop the local telecommunications sector. In February 1995, the World Bank, IMF, OECD and EBRD announced an international assistance programme to deliver over $900m to Uzbekistan over the following two years ($300m for balance of payments support, $45m for technical assistance and $580m for financing investments and export loans).

In December 1995, the IMF approved a $259m credit to Uzbekistan designed to continue market reforms. This figure consisted of the second tranche, of $74m, of its $144m Systemic Transformation Facility, the first instalment had been made available in January 1995, and $185m to function as a 15-month stand-by loan. Uzbekistan also sought to attract other sources of international finance and in September 1995 Uzbekistan became an official member of the Asia Development Bank.

Since 1996, the shift in economic policy in Uzbekistan has undermined the international programmes of assistance. Foreign private investment has also reduced significantly. In early 1998, negotiations with the IMF to establish a new stabilisation package were fruitless. Negotiations have foundered on Uzbekistan's reluctance to reverse its anti-reformist path. In particular, the government refuses to make the Som convertible and thereby abandon the system of multiple exchange rates. The government currently grants licences for favoured firms to gain access to hard currency. Other firms are usually forced to seek currency through the black market. The government is also reluctant to commit itself to trade liberalisation.

Reflecting the model of economic development that is currently in operation in Uzbekistan, the value of the Som has declined steadily over recent years. There appear to be no plans to alter the balance of economic priorities to make the national currency internationally tradable. Talking at a business conference on 6–7 November 1997 in London, the Uzbek Prime Minister Utkur Sultanov, made it clear that full convertibility will not occur in the near future. The Prime Minister noted that the government needed to marshal hard currency for the reconstruction of the country. With this set of priorities, the government wants to control spending patterns thereby preventing expenditure by the mass of the population on consumer goods.

Given the problems that the government has experienced with international financial institutions, obtaining international credits has proved difficult. In the early part of 1998 Uzbek officials raised the prospect of issuing a sovereign Eurobond but little progress has been made on this front. The poor economic fundamentals in the country and lack of transparency mean that the country is unlikely to gain a favourable credit rating, particularly following the financial crisis in Asia and the Russian Federation. Despite these problems, international institutions such as the World Bank and the Asian Development Bank continue to lend money to Uzbekistan for infrastructure, environmental and health projects and export guarantee agencies in Europe and the US provide loan assistance for the purchase of imports.[6]

SOCIAL BACKGROUND

Like other Central Asian states, the necessity of creating a dynamic and expanding economy is made more acute by the deteriorating social situation in Uzbekistan. Uzbekistan's population, which is the largest in Central Asia (23 million), is settled around the major oasis settlements of the region (Tashkent, Samarkand, Bukhara and Khiva) and the fertile region of the Fergana Valley. Sixty percent of the population lives in densely populated rural areas.

In the final decades of the Soviet Union, the population of Uzbekistan began to grow rapidly. A traditional culture and government sponsored pro-natalist policies helped to push population growth to 2.5% per annum. Despite Soviet policies that aimed to draw the rapidly rising Uzbek population from the rural areas to the towns and cities, the villagers largely remained confined to the countryside. As a result of the growth of population and high levels of hidden unemployment, the countryside began to experience increasing pressure on land and water resources.

Since independence, the social pressures in the countryside have increased significantly as population growth has continued and the state has struggled to provide welfare assistance to the population. Official figures identify approximately 44,000 registered unemployed (0.5% of the workforce) with a further 400,000 'looking for work'. In fact, the actual number of unemployed is far higher because of hidden unemployment in the countryside. In many rural areas, particularly the densely populated Fergana Valley, social pressures caused by the rising population and poverty threaten to cause unrest.

In Uzbekistan a large section of the population is below the age of 19 years, with the average age being 23.9 years. Young men in rural areas are particularly vulnerable to the social dislocation caused by the new economic conditions. In 1989 and 1990, ethnic conflict flared in the Fergana Valley as tension engendered by a struggle for resources came to a head between different groups. The minority Meskhetian population, which had managed to achieve relative economic success by occupying key economic niches in the regional economy, became the subject of violent attack by young Uzbek men frustrated by their poor prospects. The conflagration quickly transformed into an ethnic riot, forcing most of the Meskhetians to flee Uzbekistan. Unless the government is able to create the jobs and opportunities that will absorb the increasing population, the state will be required to employ increasing levels of coercion to control the population or will face increasing social unrest and conflict.

Rising levels of poverty are also contributing to increasing problems of criminality in Uzbekistan. Since the collapse of the Soviet Union, Uzbekistan has emerged as an important transhipment route for Southwest Asian narcotics heading for Russia and Europe.[7] While the government continues to profess its commitment to the fight against drugs, it made virtually no progress on counter narcotics legislation in 1997. Nevertheless, Uzbekistan's various law enforcement agencies seized 2.5 million metric tons of illicit drugs in 1997, roughly three-quarters of it opium. The problems of preventing the growth of drugs production and trade are hampered by corruption within the Customs Service and the Ministry of the Interior.

CONCLUSION

Since 1991, Uzbekistan has pursued a sporadic economic reform but throughout the period of independence the government has been reluctant to release economic performance data for the economy. In the early post-Soviet years Uzbekistan appeared to have weathered the transition period better than many of the other former Soviet republics. According to official Uzbek statistics, the recession saw GDP decline by 18% between 1991 and 1995, in Kazakhstan the equivalent was 55.9% and in Kyrgyzstan it was 54.5%. By the end of 1996, Uzbekistan claimed to have $6 billion in cumulative foreign direct investment. Economic reform while slow was proceeding and in the middle of 1995 Uzbekistan acceded to the demands of the IMF structural adjustment programme. By the end of 1995 there was some evidence that the stabilisation programme was beginning to work with monthly inflation into single digits and the fall in production slowing. At the time, the IMF forecast a small decline in real GDP in 1996 and growth of 1% in 1997.

In 1996, however, the balance of payments problems caused by a poor cotton harvest quickly developed into a far more deep-seated economic crisis. It has been suggested that the balance of payments problem was converted into a full-blown crisis by the policies of the Uzbek government.[8] Subsequently, economic development in Uzbekistan has followed a new direction, one that has seen the Uzbek economy face increasing difficulties. The new model of economic development that emerged from 1996 onwards has faced criticism from the international community.

The change of direction may not have been simply a result of the crisis of 1996 but an assertion of the underlying logic of the political economy that has operated in Uzbekistan from the very instigation of the independence. Apostolou has cast doubt upon the claim that Uzbekistan weathered the early years of independence better than its Central Asian neighbours. In particular, he challenges the notion that through a programme of gradual state-guided economic reform, Uzbekistan was able to avoid the severe output collapses of the rest of the former USSR.

Instead, Apostolou suggests that from the beginning the Uzbekistan model has seen investment directed by the state into priority sectors without regard to comparative advantage or export potential, an investment strategy not dissimilar to that of the former Soviet Union. Success in the earlier years of Uzbek independence was achieved not because of an economic model but because the Uzbeks were able to boost cotton (47.8% of exports 1992–96) and gold production (16% of exports 1992–96) and sell on world markets for hard currency.

Both of these boosts to Uzbekistan ended in 1996 when world cotton and then world gold prices slid. The failure of the cotton crop in 1996 made the situation worse, there was less cotton to sell and at a lower price. The government's repeated failure to achieve self-sufficiency in cereal production meant that large grain imports were necessitated, further raising the import bill. Together this produced a balance of payments crisis. On 19 December 1996 the IMF suspended its loan. Apostolou concludes that 'Uzbekistan's policy mix is not original, is not reformist and not a model. The combination of exchange controls and import substitution have been tried and failed in developing countries for over thirty years.'[9] The economy as a whole, remains fragile and heavily dependent on agricultural production. The Uzbeks have also adopted policies of import substitution in some sectors—gas and oil.

Apostolou's views have received support from an IMF research paper that explores the issue of 'The Uzbek Growth Puzzle'.[10] In the paper Zettelmeyer finds that the mildness of the economic transition in Uzbekistan can be accounted for by the low level of initial industrialisation, its cotton production, and its self sufficiency in energy. While the report agrees that Uzbekistan has experienced a relatively small economic decline, Zettelmeyer concludes that 'it is unlikely that the government's public investment program and import substitution strategy ... has played an important role in achieving Uzbekistan's favourable output performance'.[11] That is, Uzbekistan's economic performance did not occur because, but in spite of government policies. Moreover, if one moves beyond pure output measures of economic activity, Zettelmeyer argues that Uzbekistan could have achieved far better performance in the sphere of consumer choice and environmental improvements and the creation of a more developed private sector.

Despite strong criticism from many outside experts, the government of Uzbekistan has continued with its economic plans. Recent official reports suggest that in the first nine months of 1998 GDP increased by 4.4%, industrial output rose by 6.1% and agriculture output by 4.9%. Capital investment is reported to have risen by 13.1% and services by 12.4%. The budget deficit is also on target.[12] While such statistics should be treated with extreme caution, the official version of economic development has led some to conclude that the Uzbekistani economy is performing relatively well even though reform has been very limited.[13]

Despite the slow pace of economic change, there have been some important improvements in the Uzbek economy. Infrastructure in some sectors, notably air transport, has been improved. Telecommunications have also been upgraded, largely with assistance from foreign partners. Important investment has taken place in the energy and minerals sectors. External investment in the automotive and tobacco sectors has also had an important symbolic value. Since independence, some elements of the management of the economy have improved and fiscal discipline has tightened. The country's large natural resource base also promises to provide an important stimulus for economic development, if managed in an appropriate fashion.

Much of the early success has, however, been threatened by Karimov's reluctance to end Soviet-style controls. The expansion of state involvement in the economy after 1996 has scared off all but the most patient—and rich—foreign investors. The economy has continued to be heavily distorted by state intervention. The government is almost obsessive in its desire to control the country and the economy and continues to intervene in areas such as the lucrative foreign trade sector and in the management of enterprises.

The actions of the government create a difficult business environment for foreign firms in Uzbekistan and for Uzbekistani firms seeking to export or import goods. Firms have found that the government's control over foreign currency transactions causes particular problems.

While the current situation does not always prevent investment by large international companies such as Lonrho, Newmont, BAT and Daewoo, which are undeterred by the autocratic political regime, the extensive barriers to economic activity have discouraged small and medium size businesses, which generally employ more people. The reluctance of foreign investors to engage with the Uzbek economy has left the country dependent upon the system of commodity production imposed upon them by their old imperial masters.

While Uzbekistan has been resistant to agreeing to a new IMF programme, the prospect of good cotton harvests, and rising production in minerals and metals means that the country is to some extent sheltered from the problems facing other former Soviet economies. The rising fiscal deficit may, however, be a problem that will require international assistance. The current strategy of financing the deficit from internal revenue sources is unlikely to provide more than a short-term solution, while the financial crisis in Russia may also place increased pressure upon government finances.

In the long term, the prospects for the Uzbek economy appear unpromising, although certain sectors may well prosper. The Uzbek form of economic development remains highly vulnerable to fluctuations in the world commodity prices. More damaging is the intertwining of political and economic actors in the Uzbek system. Economic decisions are increasingly subordinated to political requirements and as a result the economy is subject to high levels of distortion. Economic policies are often intended to prevent individuals building up an economic base that would permit a political challenge to the President.

Like most other aspects of life in Uzbekistan, the economy and its prospects are closely tied to the person of President Karimov. While Karimov remains in undisputed control of the country the economy is likely to be characterised by a broad but undynamic stability. Little is being done, however, to foster the type of independent economic activity that could weather political instability. Given the close intertwining of political patronage and business networks, any uncertainty about the political future of the President is likely to translate quickly into economic difficulties.

1 James Critchlow, 'Corruption', Nationalism, and the Native Elites in Soviet Central Asia, *The Journal of Communist Studies*, vol. 4, no. 2 (June 1988), pp. 142–61 and Nancy Lubin, *Labour and Nationality in Soviet Central Asia* (Princeton, NJ: Princeton University Press, 1984).

2 *EIU Country Report: Uzbekistan*, (2nd Quarter 1998), p. 7.

3 *EIU Country Report: Uzbekistan*, (2nd Quarter 1998), p. 8.
4 *EIU Country Report: Uzbekistan*, (2nd Quarter 1998), p. 9.
5 *RFE/RL Newsline*, vol. 2, no. 224, part 1 (19 November 1998).
6 *RFE/RL Newsline*, vol. 2, no. 184, part 1 (23 September 1998) and *RFE/RL Newsline*, vol. 2, no. 123, part 1 (29 June 1998).
7 Andrew Apostolou, 'The Mistake of the Uzbek Economic Model' *Central Asia Monitor*, no. 2 (1998), pp. 19–22.
8 Apostolou, *Ibid.*, (1998), pp. 1–5.
9 Apostolou, *Ibid.*, (1998), p. 3.
10 Jeromin Zettelmeyer, *The Uzbek Growth Puzzle* (IMF Working Paper WP/98/133).
11 Zettelmeyer, *Ibid.*, (1998), p. 31.
12 *RFE/RL Newsline*, vol. 2, no. 209, part 1 (29 October 1998).
13 *RFE/RL Newsline*, vol. 2, no. 204, part 1 (21 October 1998).

Chapter 4

THE EXTERNAL POLICY OF INDEPENDENT UZBEKISTAN

INTRODUCTION

For centuries Central Asia was considered the heartland of the ancient Asian world. Its pivotal geopolitical position allowed it to play a leading role in the relations of the tribes and peoples of much of the Eurasian landmass. In early history, the territories of contemporary Uzbekistan were integrated with the political regimes and cultures to the south of the country, forming the northern border of the Persian empire. Later Central Asia became the southeastern frontier of the Mongol kingdom. In the medieval period, the region served as the link between China and Europe. During the nineteenth century, the territory of Central Asia was the subject for competition between the external imperial powers of Russia and Britain. In the contemporary period, some writers have spoken of a new 'Great Game' being fought between Iran and Turkey for influence in the region.

The submergence of Central Asia within the Russian Empire and then the Soviet Union marked the end of the political regimes of the region as independent actors in the international system. While the Central Asian republics were presented as the Asian face of Soviet Communism, and representatives from the region were included in Soviet delegations visiting developing countries, Central Asia lacked any independent capacity in the international arena. The historical role of the region as the area that linked together diverse civilisations and societies was ended and Central Asia was bound firmly to the territories to its north in the Russian heartland.

In many ways, independence for Uzbekistan at the end of 1991 led to a more fundamental change in external relations than in the spheres of domestic political and economic policy. Overnight, Tashkent was required to develop from the beginning a broad set of relations with the external world. The emergence of Uzbekistan and the other Central Asian states as independent actors in the international system has led to fundamental shifts in the interaction of states around the world with the region. The establishment of a web of external links has also been critical for Uzbekistan in the difficult years since the collapse of the Soviet state.

In seeking to develop a strong independent identity, Uzbekistan assigned a critical role to fostering new ties in the international system. Of particular significance was breaking free from Russian political, military, cultural and economic dominance through the construction of a variety of links to new partners. In the early years of independence there was often a naivety and over-optimism about what could be achieved through external policy. Uzbekistan was also hampered by the lack of experienced personnel in foreign affairs. During the Soviet period, the infrastructure of foreign relations was concentrated almost exclusively in Moscow.

Tashkent's initial approach to external relations was thus quickly tempered by the realisation that despite the important mineral resources of the region, Central Asia was not a leading priority for most of the international community, particularly its most powerful members. The focus on building relations with advanced industrial countries has therefore had to be balanced by a more realistic appreciation of the possibilities within the international system. Subsequent experience of external relations has helped Uzbekistan to develop a far more realistic and clearer set of goals than those outlined at independence. The initial emphasis on economic priorities has also been qualified by concerns about regional security.

Since independence, a complex set of interrelated factors has affected Uzbekistani external policy. Frequently these factors appear contradictory and cause problems for developing foreign policy. The drive to build a state free from the colonial past and Russian influence has meant that the Uzbekistani leadership has often promoted the symbols of a Muslim and Turkic identity. Domestic pressures have encouraged Uzbekistan to seek links to Islamic states and Turkey. At the same time, the imperative of promoting economic development has meant that Uzbekistan has looked to build good links with the West and Asia. Despite the aim of fostering new external links, geopolitical and security concerns have forced Uzbekistan to retain and sometimes rebuild relations with Russia, although, as a result, this relationship has been characterised by considerable fluctuation.

While the consolidation of national independence has been the main aim of Uzbek external policy, rather than the promotion of ideologies such as Islam, communism or pan-Turkism, the nature of Uzbek national interests has been far from clear or consistent. Domestic factors, external political and economic requirements, environmental, geopolitical and security concerns have all had an impact upon the nature and direction of external ties at different times. On occasion, Uzbekistan has presented simultaneously different faces to different audiences. The Uzbek leadership has not been afraid to present its Asian or Islamic side at the same time as promoting to the West an image of the Uzbekistani state as secular, modernising and above all stable.

Uzbekistan has, therefore, followed a course that has sought to balance seeking important economic contacts that will benefit the country with fostering political alliances appropriate to the changing geopolitical and security environment. In general terms, Tashkent has proved fairly successful in positioning itself in respect to a range of political alliances. Since independence, Tashkent has succeeded in building a positive political relationship to the United States and distancing itself from the Russian Federation to a high degree. Recently, however, the escalation of a series of issues relating to Uzbek security, particularly Afghanistan and the rise of political Islam in the region, have prompted Uzbekistan to seek a renewed but limited relationship with Russia.

The diverse range of factors driving Uzbek policy with the outside world has also meant that the country has conducted its external policy at a variety of levels. While bilateral relations have provided the core of Uzbekistan's relationship with other states, Tashkent has also joined a number of inter-state organisations. Uzbekistan operates within the context of a broader region where a complex set of issues that include the exploitation of oil and gas reserves, ethnic and religious conflict, and environmental issues, transcend state borders. The range of different contexts within which Uzbekistan external policy must operate means that it is important to consider at least four dimensions of external ties: with states in Central Asia; with regional powers; with the broader world, and; with interstate organisations.

UZBEKISTAN IN CENTRAL ASIA

Since independence, Uzbekistan has emerged as one of the leading powers in Central Asia (along with Kazakhstan). Historically, the territories and peoples of contemporary Uzbekistan played a leading role in the international life of Central Asia. Transoxiana was long considered the core of Central Asia, the location for the once powerful empires and important civilisations that dominated the region. The economic and cultural preeminence of the settled populations of this region translated into military and political power in Central Asia as a whole. The rise to dominance in the sixteenth century of Uzbek tribal groupings in Transoxiana and the creation of powerful khanates in the eighteenth century further extended this tradition.

Under Soviet rule, the territories of Uzbekistan were again assigned a leading role in Central Asia as a whole. Situated in the middle of Central Asia, Uzbekistan was central to Soviet domination of the region. From the very beginning, Uzbekistan was designed by Moscow planners to be the anchor for the rest of Soviet Central Asia. The legacy of the national delimitation of 1924–5 and its presumption of distinct ethnic identities has meant that the Uzbeks have the most developed national identity in the region. During national delimitation Uzbekistan gained the leading historic centres of Central Asia (including most of the territory of the three former khanates) and Tashkent emerged under Soviet rule as the leading city of Central Asia. The creation of the Uzbek Republic in the 1920s, thus, paved the way for the emergence of the Uzbek nation as the most populous and important Central Asia community. Throughout the Soviet period, Uzbekistan was treated as the leading republic of Central Asia.

While Uzbekistan operated as Moscow's principal agent in Central Asia, Soviet planners made sure that the republic did not grow too powerful relative to its neighbours. Uzbekistan was firmly anchored within the region and lacked significant borders with states neighbouring the USSR, except for the short frontier with Afghanistan. The reconfiguration of administrative borders within Central Asia, the creation of overlapping ethnic and social networks, and the construction of economic and infrastructure systems that straddled republican borders further served to tie Uzbekistan firmly to the rest of the region.

Moscow (through the Communist Party and the all-union state ministries) mediated the tensions engendered by the contradictions of Soviet era arrangements in Central Asia. This arrangement helped to perpetuate a leading role for the central institutions of the Soviet state. The collapse of the Soviet system and the disappearance of Moscow as a balancing force led to the emergence of a range of tensions in Central Asia focused on Uzbekistan's place in the regional order. The pre-eminence and influence of Uzbekistan has led other states of the region to talk of 'Uzbek chauvinism'. Since independence, a series of bilateral agreements and multilateral regional institutions have attempted to address many of the problems that have developed as a result of this situation.

Relations between Uzbekistan and its immediate neighbours have undergone a number of changes since the demise of the USSR. Broadly, the development of relations has passed through four principal stages. First, an idealistic commitment to regional co-operation following the collapse of the Soviet state. Second, growing rivalry and competition between the states of Central Asia. Third, the rise of forms of pragmatic co-operation in response to a range of transborder issues in the area (particularly conflict and tensions around natural resource problems). Finally, a more complex set of relations based upon diverse patterns of regional engagement and the re-emergence of a role for the Russian Federation in Central Asia.

Since independence a range of regional issues has affected Uzbekistan's relationship with the other states in Central Asia. Uzbekistan uniquely shares borders with all of the other Central Asian republics, and following the collapse of the Soviet state borders have acquired a new significance. The division of historically unified territories, economic systems, water resources, and the creation of diaspora populations have all been the source of regional tensions and together have promoted attempts to foster bilateral and regional level co-ordination. Water and ethnic issues as well as energy supplies have in particular been important factors in Uzbekistan's external policies with other Central Asian states.

Competition over water resources has been an especially significant issue in the region. Central Asia forms a single large water basin. Since the creation of independent states, management of the water resources of this basin has been split among five separate bodies where once there was one. Upstream and downstream problems have developed over water usage, with Kyrgyzstan and Tajikistan controlling the sources of much of the region's water supply. In Kazakhstan, Uzbekistan and Turkmenistan preventing the desiccation of the Aral Sea has been important. The water crisis in Central Asia is not a crisis of quantity but a crisis of distribution. Of the total water available in the Aral basin about 87% is used for agricultural purposes, 10% for industrial use, and 3% for municipal purposes. Problems over water resources have forced Uzbekistan to seek to negotiate interstate compacts and participate in a number of regional and interstate organisations.

Uzbekistan is closely tied to all of its neighbours by ethnic bonds, not least because Uzbekistan has important diaspora populations in the other republics, particularly Tajikistan and Kyrgyzstan. The rise of the diaspora Uzbeks has frequently caused acute tension along the borders with the two countries. In Uzbekistan, according to official figures the Uzbeks comprise 77% of the population and the Tajiks represent 5% (but 10–15 percent according to Tajik sources). Tajiks in Uzbekistan constitute 20.5% of the total Tajik population of the former Soviet Union. Equally significant is the large number of Uzbeks located in Tajikistan.

In Tajikistan, the Tajiks account for 62% of the population and the Uzbeks 24% (1.5 million according to Uzbek sources). Heavily Tajik-populated areas in Uzbekistan (about 3 million Tajiks) are close to the border with Tajikistan. Similarly the largely Uzbek-populated region in Tajikistan is adjacent to the Uzbek border and constitutes the most economically advanced part of Tajikistan. The Tajik minority feels vulnerable in Uzbekistan and the Uzbeks have similar feelings in Tajikistan. Uzbekistan is also home to a sizeable Slavic population, a large section of which has looked to emigrate. The important links that Uzbekistan has with other states of the region and the leading role that Uzbekistan has sought to play in Central Asia has been crucially affected by developments in Tajikistan and Afghanistan.

Tajikistan

One of Uzbekistan's central foreign policy concerns has been the civil war in Tajikistan. While the Uzbek authorities have frequently characterised the conflict as one between Islamic fundamentalists and ex-communists, Uzbek involvement has reflected the more complex nature of civil war in the region. Uzbekistan has two principal interests in Tajikistan. First, the Khojand region in the north of Tajikistan has a large Uzbek minority closely tied to Uzbekistan—both culturally and economically. Second, the emergence of an important Islamic political movement in Tajikistan has been viewed with considerable alarm in Tashkent.

The Khojand region traditionally dominated the politics of Tajikistan, supplying the republic's top leaders from the late 1930s until the outbreak of the civil war. The close involvement of Uzbeks from this region in the top politics of the republic helped offset any concerns that the Uzbek minority might have about being located outside the borders of the Uzbek Republic. The disintegration of the Tajik state in the early 1990s posed a threat to the balance of ethnic and political forces that had been established in the area and threatened to destabilise the border situation with Uzbekistan.

Alarmed about instability caused by the conflict in Tajikistan and about possible secessionist movements among the Uzbeks of Tajikistan, Tashkent has played an active role in seeking to protect the interests of the Khojand region. In May 1992 Tashkent was pivotal in securing a Khojand-Kulob political alliance as the Tajikistani state collapsed in the face of conflict. This grouping emerged as the dominant factor in the politics of Dushanbe, signaled by the election by the Tajik parliament of President Rakhmonov in 1992. Uzbekistan also helped ensure that the new grouping was backed with military support.

From 1992, however, the Kulobis staged a series of elections culminating in the popular election of Rakhmonov as president, after which they drove the representatives of the Khojand region (including Uzbeks) from central and local political positions. Relations between the Khojandis and Kulobis worsened as the former came to perceive of themselves as subjects to discrimination.

Concerned by this development, Karimov began to support inclusion of some elements of the opposition movement in a coalition government, including the Islamic Renaissance Party, as a means to weaken Kulob pre-eminence. In April 1995, Karimov met Akbar Turajonzoda, the first deputy leader of the United Tajik Opposition (UTO), who had been the highest Islamic authority in Tajikistan until his dismissal by the Dushanbe regime in 1993. The UTO began to support the allocation of places to representatives from Khojand in the peace negotiations and in any future government.

Even before the peace process was developed, however, the Khojandis were becoming dissatisfied with the Kulobi political administration, and in May 1996 and January 1997 anti-Kulob demonstrations were held in several northern cities of Tajikistan. Relations between the Tajik government and the representatives of the Khulob region were further strained when a prison riot took place in Khojand from 14–17 April 1997 and an assassination attempt was made on Tajikistani President Imomali Rakhmonov while he was visiting the region on 30 April 1997. Both of these events led to a crackdown in the north of the country in 1997.

After prolonged negotiations followed by the conclusion of a ceasefire in December 1996, Rakhmonov and the leader of the UTO, Sayed Abdullo Nuri, met in Moscow in late June 1997 to sign a General Agreement on Peace and National Accord. Representatives of the Khojand region were not included in the peace process. Stating that there was no mechanism by which to enforce the Accord, Uzbekistan was the only one of the eight guarantor states that refused to sign the inter-Tajik agreement (the other states being Iran, Russian, Pakistan, Turkmenistan, Kyrgyzstan, Kazakhstan and Afghanistan). Two months later, however, Uzbekistan changed its position and agreed to become a guarantor of the peace process.

Alarm in Tashkent about the peace agreement reflected the fact that the Khojand-based National Revival Movement (NRM) was excluded from the peace process. The NRM is chaired by Tajikistan's ex-prime minister Adbumalik Abdullojanov and has the support of Tashkent. Despite the importance of the Khojand region, particularly its economic significance, the region was initially excluded from the peace settlement and the leaders of the region became in effect an opposition to the Rakhmonov government. In April 1998, the NRM again requested to be included in the peace process but reportedly was denied access.

While relations between Uzbekistan and Tajikistan have often been tense because of Uzbekistan's political support for the Khojand region, friction has also stemmed from the suspicion that Tashkent has played a more direct role in the events in Tajikistan. In October 1997 Tashkent was linked to an armed uprising in western Tajikistan close to the border with Uzbekistan. Reportedly, Colonel Mahmud Khudoiberdiev led the uprising. A member of the Central Committee of the Tajik Communist Party and a former officer in the Soviet army, Mahmud Khudoiberdiev is an important figure in Tajikistan. Khudoiberdiev is half Uzbek and has strong support from the Uzbek community that makes up one third of the population of Khojand. In February 1996 and August 1997 the rebel commander also mounted rebellions. The commander's main areas of support are located in Kurgan-Tyube and Khojand regions. On all occasions, Khudoiberdiev was reported to have invaded from camps based inside Uzbekistan.

Relations between Dushanbe and Tashkent underwent a crisis in late 1998 as the result of a serious rebellion in northern Tajikistan. On 4 November Khudoiberdiev seized control of most of the north of

Tajikistan. Khudoiberdiev demanded from Dushanbe that no less than 40 percent of jobs throughout the country's government structure should be given to natives of the north. Within a few days, the Tajik authorities had managed to put the rebellion down and the rebel leader fled. The International Red Cross reported that there were some 2,000 causalities.

Dushanbe believes that responsibility for planning the uprising lies not only with Khudoiberdiev but also with Tajikistan's former Prime Minister Abdulmalik Abdullajonov, and a number of other officials, who live in Tashkent. They all originally hail from the northern districts of Tajikista and are prominent in the opposition to the regime in Dushanbe. Abdullajonov broke with the current rulers of Dushanbe when he decided to run in the presidential elections against Rakhmonov and he gained up to 93% of the votes in his native region.

The Tajikistani authorities also believe that Tashkent supported the actions of Abdullajonov and Khudoiberdiev. Speaking to the Tajikistani parliament in November 1998, President Rakhmonov accused the leadership of neighbouring Uzbekistan of helping the armed uprising in his country, which he termed 'an attempted coup'. He argued that '... The military coup in the north of Tajikistan was thoroughly planned military aggression and a crude intrusion in the internal affairs of sovereign Tajikistan by Uzbekistan'. 'We have proof that Uzbek President Islam Karimov completely supports the organiser of the Tajik mutiny, former Prime Minister Abdulmalik Abdullajonov. By organising coups and helping rebels, the Uzbek leadership wants to take the whole of Tajikistan under its control'.[1]

The Uzbek Foreign Minister Abdulaziz Kamilov announced on 11 November that his country had not given permission to the leaders of the failed revolt in northern Tajikistan either to enter or to settle in Uzbekistan. But Kamilov admitted that the borders between the two countries are porous.[2] At a press conference in Tashkent on 30 November Uzbek Prime Minister Islam Karimov denied his country had any role in the rebellion in northern Tajikistan. He said that the fighting in Tajikistan was the result of 'an inter-clan struggle for power'.[3]

The peace agreement in Tajikistan is fragile because it represents only the interests of the Rakhmonov regime and the UTO and does not include the interests of the 'Third Force'. Tashkent continues to support the inclusion in the peace settlement of representatives from Khojand. The coming to power of the pro-Islamic members of the

Tajik opposition has, however, given Tashkent an incentive to build a closer relationship with the Tajikistani President Rakhmonov. Uzbekistan's initial support for Rakhmonov was guided by alarm about the emergence of an Islamic political movement within the opposition. Despite the attempt to use the UTO to pressure Rakhmonov into incorporating representatives from Khojand into the peace settlement, Tashkent continues to be concerned about the inclusion of Islamic elements from the UTO within the peace process.

Inspite of the on-going difficult relationship between Tajikistan and Uzbekistan, the two presidents have sought to moderate their hostility. In January 1998 the Tajikistani President made a 'working visit' to Tashkent at which the status of the Russian troops in Tajikistan was discussed. In February 1998 a high level delegation from Uzbekistan, including the Prime Minister Utkur Sultanov, went to Dushanbe for the first time in five years. Sultanov announced that Tajikistan's debt to Uzbekistan had been rescheduled and the possibility of a Karimov visit was discussed. On 30 June 1998 Rakhmonov paid a one-day visit to Tashkent and noted that 'We are starting a new page in our relations'.[4] Following the November uprising, relations again cooled but on 8 January 1999 the Uzbek president and Tajik Prime Minister Yahye Azimov met in Tashkent to discuss trade and economic co-operation. The two sides agreed on a formula to resume natural gas supplies from Uzbekistan to Tajikistan. It was the first official meeting between Tajik and Uzbek officials since the Tajik President accused Uzbekistan of habouring mutineers who had tried to seize territory in northern Tajikistan in early November.

Despite the frictions generated over the region of Khojand, Uzbekistan has sought to foster good relations with Dushanbe because Tajikistan is often seen as Russia's 'last protectorate' in Central Asia. Uzbekistan would like to replace Russia as the key actor in the Tajik conflict. Russia is able to use the conflict in Tajikistan as justification for a continued Russian military presence in the region, which Tashkent would like to see withdrawn. Uzbekistan's resistance towards Russian involvement in the region has, however, been moderated by events in Afghanistan.

Afghanistan

In April 1992 the Najibullah regime in Kabul was overthrown by the *mujahidin* coalition and Afghanistan was declared an Islamic republic.

This event significantly strengthened regional Islamic movements and ethnic competition and exerted new pressures on Central Asia, especially on Tajikistan. The regional implications of the long running conflict in Afghanistan escalated quickly when the Taliban captured Kabul in the autumn of 1996. In response to this development Uzbekistan bolstered its military presence along its border with Afghanistan.

Initially, Tashkent attempted to establish the regions of the north of Afghanistan as a buffer zone. At a summit of Central Asian heads of state and the Russian Prime Minister Victor Chernomyrdin in October 1996, Karimov called for support for General Abdurrashid Dostum and his forces. Dostum, an ethnic Uzbek warlord in the north of Afghanistan, received assistance from Uzbekistan including what many people believe was military assistance. In May 1997 the Taliban overran Dostum's forces and entered Mazar-i-Sharif, prompting Tashkent to close the border. Following further fighting the Taliban reached the border with Uzbekistan leading Karimov to call for the creation of an 'international contact group' to negotiate a solution to the war. The contact group would have operated under the umbrella of the UN and the Islamic Conference Organisation. The attempt to develop a multilateral response—including the US—rather than relying on Russian military power appeared to reflect Uzbekistan's continuing desire to keep Russia out of the region.

In August 1998 the Taliban once again overran Mazar-i-Sharif, defeating opposition forces and pushing on to conquer most of the northern territories of Afghanistan. What appeared to be the final defeat for Dostum caused considerable alarm in Uzbekistan, and Central Asia more generally. President Karimov visited the Uzbek-Afghan border on 15 August and met senior military officials. The foreign and defence ministers of Kazakhstan, Kyrgyzstan, Tajikistan and Uzbekistan met in Tashkent on 22–23 August 1998 to discuss regional security in the light of recent advances by the Taliban. President Karimov spoke of the threat to Uzbekistan posed by the Taliban when addressing Uzbekistan's parliament on 28 August.[5] On September 22 the Uzbek Defence Minister, Khikmatulla Tursunov, accused Afghanistan of being a centre for international terrorism, religious extremism, and worldwide drug trafficking. He said that events in the country 'threaten to spiral out of control' and threaten neighbouring states.[6]

The Taliban victories in 1998 also helped to accelerate a limited rapprochement between Russia and Uzbekistan. Tashkent's concerns about the rise of Islamic fundamentalism in Central Asia had already provided the basis for a common agenda with Moscow. The apparent security threat posed by the Taliban and the fact that this threat came in the form of a radical Islamic movement further consolidated the new Russian-Uzbek relationship. As the Taliban advanced on Mazar-i-Sharif, the head of the Russian General Staff and Russian first Deputy Foreign Minister flew to Tashkent to discuss developments. Both sides spoke of the right to take measures to preserve the integrity of the borders of the Commonwealth of Independent States (CIS).

RELATIONS WITH REGIONAL POWERS

Uzbekistan's geopolitical position and its landlocked status have ensured that relations with a set of regional powers have been critical to Tashkent's ability to foster and consolidate independence. While the Russian Federation remains the leading regional power in Central Asia, since the fall of the Soviet Union a variety of other states, including Turkey, Iran, Pakistan and China, have come to play new and important roles in the region.

The Russian Federation

As the former colonial power in Central Asia, the Russian Federation's relationship to Uzbekistan has often been difficult. A central aim of Uzbek policy has been to reduce the role of the Russian Federation in Central Asia, however, this aim has been undermined by ethnic, economic and security issues that have forced Tashkent to retain important links to Moscow. These contradictory imperatives have led to a number of fluctuations in the relationship between Russia and Uzbekistan.

In the early years of independence, with its priorities focused on the West and internal issues Moscow paid little attention to Central Asia. In the final years of the USSR it was widely believed in Russia that Central Asia had become a net economic burden on the Soviet Union. Building new ties to the region were nor viewed as a priority for Moscow. Economic links reduced and new ones were only infrequently established. Russian companies rarely take part in large-scale ventures in Uzbekistan, in part owing to Russian legislation making it tougher for Russian citizens to invest private capital in the economies of foreign states.[7]

Uzbekistan initially adopted a cautiously positive relationship to Russia and Russian inspired institutions such as the CIS. Karimov called for a NATO-style military element to the CIS, separate armies that pool their resources. These declarations set the stage for an important CIS meeting on 15 May 1992 in Tashkent where delegates signed a number of agreements culminating in a mutual defence treaty between Russia, Uzbekistan, Kazakhstan, Turkmenistan, Tajikistan, and Armenia. Under the terms of the treaty, aggression against one signatory is considered to be aggression against all.

A set of events at the beginning of 1992 prompted the first significant shift in Uzbek attitudes towards the CIS. In this period it became clear that Russia would be adopting a domestic economic reform package based upon liberalisation regardless of the implications for the other Soviet states. The resulting rise in prices triggered student riots in Tashkent. Karimov complained that Russia was not behaving like an equal partner. Karimov and his central bank chairmen stated that if the CIS did not operate as a body for true joint policy-making, Uzbekistan would be forced to introduce its own national currency.

The rhetoric directed against Moscow from Uzbekistan increased significantly after Russia attempted to put increased pressure on rouble-zone members in 1993 through the introduction of a new rouble. In response, Uzbekistan introduced its own currency, the Som on 15 November 1993. The currency change also caused tensions within Uzbekistan as the local Russian population realised how distant from the Russian Federation they had become. In March 1996 after the Russian State Duma passed a resolution declaring the dissolution of the USSR legally invalid, relations with Uzbekistan again deteriorated.

President Karimov has often appeared particularly opposed to a continuing Russian military presence in Central Asia. Russia, however, has developed defence and foreign policy doctrines towards Central Asia that justify military intervention in the region, particularly when Russian security and the rights of ethnic Russians are threatened. Moscow has also claimed the right to defend the old borders of the USSR. Uzbekistan has rejected such claims and refused to sign the Treaty for the Defence of the CIS External Borders in May 1995.

In order to counter the previous reliance on Russian military capabilities, Uzbekistan quickly developed its own military forces following independence. The numbers in the Uzbek army are disputed but are approximately 40–70,000, with around 100,000 reservists. Uzbekistan has moved rapidly to increase the percentage of ethnic Uzbek officers in the armed forces. At independence only 6% of the officers were Uzbek in the Slavic dominated upper echelons of the national armed forces. By 1997, the figure was closer to 85%. Unlike most other Central Asia states, Uzbekistan does not have Russian military bases on its soil.

By the mid-1990s, Russia's position towards Uzbekistan was beginning to change as Moscow sought new arrangements with the Central Asian states, particularly in response to the drive to develop the region's hydrocarbon reserves. In addition, a group composed of representatives and industrialists from Russian textile regions, who wanted access to Uzbek cotton, and some figures in the foreign policy and defence establishments, who felt Central Asia was important to Russian interests, began to lobby for a more active relationship with the region. The appointment of Evgenii Primakov as foreign minister in January 1996, a Middle East expert, was interpreted as a shift in Moscow to a more southern strategy. In fact some of Primakov's first official visits were to Central Asia, including stops in Uzbekistan in January and February 1996. But, by then Uzbekistan had moved some distance in breaking its previous dependence on Moscow.

Primakov was only able to conclude one of the agreements he intended during his February visit to Tashkent. Unsigned agreements included the important issue of the status of the Russians in Uzbekistan. Despite the difficult political relationship, Russia remains Uzbekistan's leading trading partner, and Uzbekistan is ranked fourth in terms of Russia's trade. In recognition of the importance of the Uzbek economy for Russia, Russia has taken a number of initiatives to promote business links. In December 1997 Prime Minister Chernomyrdin undertook a visit to Tashkent to discuss future economic co-operation.

Although Uzbekistan has tried to limit its relationship with the Russian Federation, conflicts in Afghanistan and Tajikistan forced Tashkent to realise the continuing importance of the Russian Federation as a guarantor of stability and borders in the region. Recently, the interest that Russia and Uzbekistan share in suppressing radical Islam has provided an important stimulus for a form of rapprochement between the two ex-Soviet republics. Attending a conference of CIS interior ministers in Tashkent in 1998, the Russian Interior Minister, Sergei Stepashin, argued fundamentalism is 'a CIS problem' and he noted that 'expressions of fundamentalism... or Wahhabism...have become a serious issue throughout the CIS'.[8] Russia has proposed that the CIS be used to combat the rise of Islamic fundamentalism.

In October 1998, President Yeltsin undertook a brief trip to Central Asia, including a visit to Uzbekistan. The two-day visit in Tashkent was the first visit by Yeltsin as Russian President to Uzbekistan, perhaps reflecting the warming relations between the two countries. A critical issue for discussion was the Taliban. The two presidents signed an agreement promising aid in the event that one of their countries was attacked. President Rakhmonov had already signed the document, which also included reference to cooperating with international organisations to help stabilise the situation in Tajikistan. Yeltsin and Karimov also concluded an accord on economic co-operation over the coming decade.[9]

Russian Deputy Prime Minister Gennadii Kulik was in Tashkent, 8–9 January 1999 for a meeting of the Russian-Uzbek intergovernmental commission on economic cooperation and for talks with various Uzbek officials around deepening economic ties. Despite the apparent progress on further economic co-operation, the political relationship between Uzbekistan and Russia continues to be fragile. Later in the same month as the success of the Russian-Uzbek intergovernmental commission, Uzbekistan announced that it would not renew its involvement in the CIS Collective Security Treaty beyond April 1999. The Uzbek Foreign Ministry noted, however, that this decision will not affect bilateral agreements on cooperation with Russia.[10]

Turkey

For decades Turkey had no significant interest in the Turkic populations of Central Asia. The founder of Turkey—Kemal Ataturk—had made it a basic principal that the new country would eschew pan-Turkic or pan-Islamic policies. In particular, this meant that Turkey should avoid entanglement in the affairs of the newly established Bolshevik state. From the foundation of the Turkish state, the external orientation of Ankara was thus westward and modernising. The collapse of the Soviet Union changed the historic thrust of Turkish external policy. Problems associated with Turkey's ambition to join the European Union and uncertainty about Turkey's place in the western order once it lost its position as the frontier with communism meant that turning east seemed an ideal means to carve out a new Turkish identity to fit the changed international circumstances.

Under President Turgut Ozal, the apparent rediscovery of millions of Turkic people in the East was presented as representing new opportunities for Turkey in the post-communist era. Official relations between Turkey and Uzbekistan seemed to blossom when in mid-December 1991 Karimov visited Ankara and Turkey became the first state to recognise Uzbekistan's independence. Nine documents on co-operation were signed during the visit. Turkish airlines began flights to Tashkent. The Uzbek-Turkish relationship reached its zenith in March 1992 when the Turkish Prime Minister visited Tashkent to open the new Turkish embassy. He promised \$500 million of credits and signed various agreements on investment. The largest event in Turkish-Uzbek relations was the Ankara summit of leaders of Turkic-speaking states on 30–31 October 1992. This meeting seemed to presage the resurrection of some idea of Greater Turkestan when the leaders signed a document on political and economic co-operation; what became known as the Ankara Doctrine.

The emergence of independent Central Asian states has, however, presented problems as well as opportunities for Turkey. While the Turkish model of secular development was initially attractive to Uzbekistan, the idea that Turkey would emerge as a guiding state in the region was not welcomed. The perception that Turkey was seeking to replace Russia as the dominant power or new 'big brother' in Central Asia was reinforced when some writers began to use the image of the Great Game to describe Turkey's role in the region. The new Great Game was viewed as a clash between a secular modernising Turkey, with the stress upon the ethnic and religious affinities between Turkey and the Central Asian states, versus Islamic Iran, with its claim of Persian cultural and historic links to the region.

In fact, the initial promise of developing a close relationship with Turkey has not been fulfilled. Although the 'Turkish' model was initially hailed by Karimov, Turkey was unable to deliver the expected investment and financial assistance. Extensive cultural links have been set in place and Turkey has played a leading role in the telecommunications sector, the provision of educational opportunities and the training of diplomatic and military personnel, but links have not developed as originally hoped. Also the natural bonds that seemed to provide the basis for relations with Ankara have proved to be far weaker than originally supposed.

The emergence of a powerful Islamic movement in Turkey also did much to dent the Turkish secular model. In August 1997 Karimov decided to withdraw most of the Uzbekistani students studying in Turkey for fear they were being influenced by Islamic activists. Relations between Turkey and Uzbekistan began to improve following the replacement of the Islamic government in Ankara led by Necmettin Erbakan. The importance of Turkey as a transit route for east-west trade through Central Asia, particularly oil and gas, has, however, fostered a new relationship based upon economic interest. At a meeting on the sidelines of the 75th anniversary celebrations of the founding of the Republic of Turkey in Ankara on 29 October, President Karimov (along with the presidents of Turkey, Georgia, Azerbaijan, and Kazakhstan), signed a declaration affirming his support for routing the main export pipeline for Caspian oil from Baku to the Turkish Mediterranean port of Ceyhan.[11]

Despite these important changes, Tashkent has nevertheless been reluctant to be seen as part of a Turkish sphere of influence. Turkey has also remained cautious over its approach to the region based upon broader political and strategic calculations. Ankara has been anxious not to antagonise Russia because of the wider aims of developing hydrocarbon resources and building good ties with the Transcaucasus region.

Iran, Pakistan, and China

In the early years of Uzbekistan's independence Iran appeared to emerge as the principal rival to Turkey for influence in Central Asia. Originally, Tehran sought to build links with Tajikistan reflecting the historic cultural, linguistic and religious ties between Iran and the Tajik population. Iran's relations with the states of Central Asia have, however, been complicated. The emergence of an Islamic political movement in Tajikistan also appeared to attract support from Iran. Tajikistan did not develop as the important force in Central Asia that was once hoped. The idea of a greater Tajikistan based upon the cultural and historic bonds of the former empires centred upon Bukhara and Samarkand, quickly disappeared as Tajikistan descended into civil war and chaos.

Uzbekistan has been hesitant to build close economic or political ties with Iran, and has developed links more slowly than other Central Asian states. From the earliest years of independence, President Karimov was highly critical of the Iranian Islamic state. He was particularly alarmed by reports that Iran had provided support for Islamic groups in Tajikistan in 1992–3.

When the early Iranian approach failed to deliver the expected results in terms of relations to Central Asia, Iran adopted a more conservative and non-interventionist policy towards the region. Tehran has tended to focus upon economic links rather than promoting Islam in the region. Iran, in particular, has tried to foster good links with Kazakhstan and Turkmenistan in order to secure a common approach to oil and gas issues. Uzbekistan has played a lesser role in Iran's relations with the region. While bilateral ties to the Central Asian states have been largely built on the basis of economic interest, Iran has on occasion attempted to politicise the interstate Economic Cooperation Organisation (see below).

Islam has been a particular problem in relations between Uzbekistan and Iran. While Iran has sought to downplay its Islamic identity in external relations in recent years, the anti-Islam campaign launched in Uzbekistan in 1998 caused unease in Tehran. In May 1998 Iranian television broadcast a programme critical of Karimov arguing that Karimov has been trying to form an anti-Islamic alliance with Russia and Tajikistan for some time.[12]

Pakistan's relationship to Uzbekistan has been limited since the demise of the Soviet Union. This, despite the fact that Pakistan initially held high hopes for its links to Central Asia. Pakistan sought allies in the region because of its troubled relationship with the United States following the end of the communist era. Links to the Central Asian muslim states on the basis of pan-Islamic solidarity were also seen as way to counter India.

From the beginning, Pakistan emphasised the economic dimension of its relationship to Central Asia. Pakistan was particularly keen to build up transport infrastructure as a means to promote development within the territories of the Economic Cooperation Organisation. The major advantage that Pakistan offers to the land-locked Central Asian states is that it provides the shortest route to seaport facilities, at Karachi. Pakistan has also sought energy supplies and cotton from the region and has offered credit and goods in return.

Although Pakistan has established some joint ventures with Uzbekistan, Pakistan's involvement in the region has been severely curtailed by its role in the war in Afghanistan and lack of financial resources available for investment and loans. It is widely believed that Pakistan was behind the creation of the Taliban and continues to supply the movement with materiel. Uzbekistan has been particularly critical of Pakistan and tension between the two countries surfaced over the Taliban at the summit of the Economic Cooperation Organisation in May 1997. Pakistan has promoted the Taliban in part to counter the fear of a possible break up of Afghanistan. The disintegration of Afghanistan would be likely to threaten the territorial integrity of Pakistan because of calls to establish a state based upon 'Great Pashtunistan'. The rising political power of Islamic movements in Pakistan is also viewed with concern in Tashkent.

Since independence the link between China and Central Asia has changed fundamentally with the former confrontational relationship replaced by one of cooperation. China has emerged as an important force in Central Asia and is likely to have a key role in the future development of the region. China has become the leading trade partner for the states of the region after Russia. To date, however, Chinese priorities in the region have been focused on Kazakhstan and Kyrgyzstan because of former disputes about border demarcation and concern about transborder Muslim separatist movements.

Chinese contacts with Uzbekistan have been primarily economic, and China has become a significant trading partner for Uzbekistan. China is likely to become particularly important for Uzbekistan if moves to develop east-west transport links are pursued. During his April 1994 visit to Uzbekistan, Chinese premier Li Peng spoke of reopening the old silk route through Uzbekistan but he stressed that Chinese involvement was not intended to counter the interests of any other party. China, like Turkey, has been reluctant to upset Russia over its involvement in Central Asia because of a range of other Sino-Russian interests.

UZBEKISTAN IN THE WORLD

The Western Powers

The Uzbekistani leadership initially gave relations with the western powers the highest priority. Engagement with the West was seen as critical for the project of developing the domestic economy. Tashkent also sought access to international financial institutions and the credits available from these organisations for macroeconomic stabilisation, investment and for cleaning up environmental problems in the region. While economic interests were the main factor behind the drive to forge links with western states, Tashkent also hoped that the West would be in a position to provide Uzbekistan and Central Asia more generally with some sort of security guarantees.

While western interest in Central Asia has risen considerably since the end of the Soviet state, engagement remains limited. Western economic attention has been focused upon the hydrocarbon sector and mineral extraction. The relatively small size of hydrocarbon deposits in Uzbekistan means, however, that the country has been of comparatively little interest to western energy companies. In this respect, Uzbekistan has lost ground to Kazakhstan. Politically, western concern with the region has also been limited, focusing mostly on the issue of the drugs trade, nuclear disarmament and the possibility of the rise of political Islam. Western relations have often appeared to be driven more by a desire to block potential rivals gaining influence in the region, particularly the Russian Federation and Iran, than with developing an active alliance with Uzbekistan. Despite the limited nature of western engagement with the region, Uzbekistan has been relatively successful at developing a positive relationship with the United States and has emerged as an important partner for European states in the region, particularly Germany.

The United States

The rapid emergence of an authoritarian regime, the suppression of all opposition, and the violation of human rights in Uzbekistan initially clouded Tashkent's relationship with the United States. From 1992 until 1995 US-Uzbekistani relations were characterised by tension. President Karimov was denied permission by the US authorities to travel to a UN session in New York and Vice-President Al Gore avoided going to Tashkent during a visit to Central Asia. It was only in June 1996 that Karimov was received in the White House, far later than other Central Asia leaders.

From 1995 the relationship with the United States began to change. As a result of this shift, Uzbekistan emerged as a strategic partner for the United States in the region. The US change of policy was prompted by a variety of economic and security concerns. Uzbekistan began to be perceived as critical to the US because of the important hydrocarbon and mineral resources in the region and the conflicts in Tajikistan and Afghanistan. In contrast to other regimes of the region, Uzbekistan appeared to be a stable, pro-western and powerful state that could be used to protect western interests. Within the new US relationship to Uzbekistan, human rights has been replaced by economic and security issues.

Changing perceptions of Uzbekistan in Washington were also affected by Uzbekistan's external policies. Uzbekistan's resistance to Russian influence in the region was regarded as a positive factor by some US policy makers. Uzbekistan has been cautious on relations with Iran, cultivated links primarily with the West rather than Islamic countries, and has sought good relations with NATO. The chairman of NATO's military council Klaus Naumann visited Uzbekistan on 2 July 1998 and was warm in his support for Uzbekistan's involvement in military exercises.[13] Uzbekistan has also been supportive of Israel in the United Nations. Uzbekistan has thus sought to position itself as a key regional state for US interests, similar to the role performed by Turkey and Israel in the Middle East, a relationship that is premised upon the United States emerging as chief guarantor of Uzbekistan's independent foreign policy and international security.[14]

On the basis of Uzbekistan's drive to present itself as a reliable and positive partner of western states, Korean and Japanese involvement in Uzbekistan has risen. The Asian countries have made some high profile investments and also provided aid and loans to Tashkent. The political role of the industrialised Asian states in Central Asia has, however, been limited.

Interstate organisations

While the central thrust of Uzbekistan's external relations has been focused upon strengthening its national independence through bilateral arrangements, Uzbekistan has joined a number of regional and multilateral organisations. With the exception of the Turkmen president, Saparmurad Niyazov, Karimov has, however, been the most reluctant of the Central Asian leaders to participate in supra-state structures. Uzbekistan has been especially resistant to extensive involvement in organisations dominated by the Russian Federation.

The Commonwealth of Independent States (CIS)

The CIS was originally intended to be an important interstate organisation that would replace some of the functions of the Soviet state. On 8 December 1991 the heads of the three Slavic states (Russia, Ukraine and Belarus) met to form a commonwealth. The Central Asian states were concerned to prevent the development of a purely Slavic bloc and moved quickly to be included in the new interstate structures. The Central Asian states convened in Ashkhabad four days after the Slavic leaders had met and decided to press for membership of the

Commonwealth. On 21 December 1991 eleven republics from the former Soviet Union met to announce the establishment of the CIS.

Despite initial support for the CIS, Uzbek resistance to the institution has steadily grown. At the heart of the tensions within the CIS have been the diverse interests and aims of the organisation's membership. Russia has sought a far more political role for the Commonwealth, while many other states have seen the CIS more in terms of general co-ordination. Uzbekistan has been opposed to any ideas designed to promote further integration, especially when coming from Russia. Uzbekistani resistance to the CIS has grown with each new Russian initiative to develop common CIS foreign policy and domestic agendas. At the CIS meeting in Moldova in October 1997 Russia was denounced by various participants including Uzbekistan and none of the agreements or statements were signed.

At a press conference with President Nazarbayev of Kazakhstan in late 1998, Karimov said 'the structures of the Commonwealth should be seriously reformed'. He argued that the main aim of the CIS should be 'widening the economic interaction' of member states. He noted, however, that despite support for a restricted role for the CIS, both Kazakhstan and Uzbekistan are 'strategic partners' of Russian President Yeltsin.[15] In early 1999, Uzbekistan announced it would not be renewing its involvement in the CIS Collective Security Treaty beyond April, thereby further weakening the political and military identity of the CIS. Tashkent was reported to be alarmed about Moscow's policies in the Caucasus, particularly supplying weaponry to Armenia, and the concern that a similar agreement would be signed with Tajikistan.[16]

Uzbekistan's position towards the CIS has undergone a steady evolution from enthusiastic support to extreme skepticism. The CIS has, however, played an important role in Uzbekistan's external policy. Although criticising the CIS and Russia in particular, Uzbekistan has used the organisation as a forum for discussions with other states and as a means to forge coalitions to block Russian initiatives toward further integration.

The Central Asian Union (CAU)

Despite the search for new partners and allies outside Central Asia, there has been a growing recognition within Uzbekistan that increased co-ordination among the Central Asian states is required because t hey share many problems. As early as the founding meeting of the CIS in December 1991, Kazakhstani President Nursultan

Nazarbaev proposed the formation of a Turkic or Central Asian Union. While the idea may have been a bargaining chip to encourage Russia to support the inclusion of the Central Asian states in the CIS, the idea of integration has continued to find support in the region.

In a meeting in Bishkek the following April, the possibility of further economic cooperation was discussed but enthusiasm for the project began to ebb as it became clear that Uzbekistan would most likely dominate any new structure. Further expressions of interest in co-operation between the Central Asian states were made in Tashkent in January 1993 in response to the conflict in Tajikistan and the environmental problems of the Aral Sea.

After the Central Asian states were ejected from the rouble zone in 1993, events seemed to be pushing the states of the region closer together. President Nazarbaev proposed a Eurasian Union but competition with Uzbekistan grew. In response to Nazarbaev's initiative, which stressed the common links between the European territories and peoples of the former Soviet Union and those of Central Asia, President Karimov proposed integration within Central Asia under the slogan 'Turkestan Our Common Home'.

In January 1994, Uzbekistan signed an agreement with Kyrgyzstan and Kazakhstan that aimed to create a 'common economic space' by the end of the century. The aims and structures of the Central Asian Union (CAU) included an Interstate Council comprised of the three presidents, and further councils for their prime ministers, foreign ministers and defence ministers. The Central Asian Bank for Cooperation and Development was set up in Almaty with the intention of providing funding for joint projects. A permanent working body, the Executive Committee of the Inter-state Council was also established.

At a meeting of the five Central Asian states in January 1998 the possibility of enlarging the Central Asian Union by including Tajikistan and Turkmenistan was discussed. A protocol admitting Tajikistan to the CAU was signed on 26 March 1998. At the same time, the presidents of Kazakhstan, Kyrgyzstan, Russia and Belarus admitted Tajikistan to the quadripartite CIS Customs Union in April 1998, perhaps signaling an attempt to bloc Uzbekistan's drive to draw Tajikistan away from Russia.

The CAU has evolved only slowly reflecting different understandings and competing ambitions. Kyrgyzstan, for example, has been forced to maneuver between Kazakhstan and Uzbekistan because of its lack of natural resources and the ethnic problems in the south. The form of economic development that has been selected by the different states of Central Asia has also caused tensions within the CAU. Whereas Kazakhstan has adopted a more liberal economic policy, Uzbekistan continues to follow a largely autarkic approach to economic management.

In the early years of independence, a strong rivalry emerged between Kazakhstan and Uzbekistan over leadership in Central Asia. While President Nazarbayev promoted his vision of a 'Eurasian Union', President Karimov countered with his idea of 'Turkestan Our Common Home'. In recent times, there has been a partial rapprochement between the two leaders reflecting the emergence of elements of a common agenda. In October 1998, President Nazarbayev wrapped up his first official visit to Uzbekistan by signing an 'eternal friendship' treaty with his Uzbek counterpart. A series of economic agreements were also concluded.[17]

The development of the CAU has also had to confront a number of structural problems. The volume of trade between the Central Asian states is significantly smaller that their trade with states outside the region. The economic and technological backwardness of the Central Asian countries forces them to base their development upon the advanced economies. The economies of the Central Asian states are also competitive rather than complementary; they tend to produce the same sort of products.

Competition between Uzbekistan, Kazakhstan and Russia has made any development of the CAU difficult. In March 1996 a customs union brought together Russia, Belarus, Kazakhstan and Kyrgyzstan. Uzbekistan refused to join the Union and instead continues to support the CAU. Uzbekistan has been reluctant to join the CIS Customs Union afraid it will lock the Central Asian states into dependence on Russia. In order to counter the role of the Russian dominated CIS and Customs Union, Uzbekistan has argued for the creation of mechanisms to foster economic co-operation between the states of Central Asia.

In fact, the CAU has made only modest progress in its aim of promoting economic integration within Central Asia and an attempt was made to reinvigorate the structures in 1996. The main outcome of the meeting was the creation of the joint peacekeeping battalion 'Centrasbat' under the aegis of the UN. Uzbekistan has supported strongly the creation of the Centrasbat because it fits well with

Tashkent's broader aim of integrating into NATO's Partnership for Peace (PFP) initiative. Uzbekistan has been the most active Central Asian member of the NATO programme and has taken part in a number of PFP sponsored peacekeeping exercises and the major military exercise Centrasbat 97 in Uzbekistan and Kazakhstan.

There have also been some areas of limited success. The main areas of progress within the CAU have been transportation, communications, the use of fuel, energy and water resources, and the construction and use of pipelines serving the Central Asian region. An important purpose of the CAU has been to develop a common approach to oil and gas exports that will bypass Russia. A conference of the Central Asian Union on reforms to the CAU was held in Bishkek on 2–3 June 1998. It was announced that a council of heads of the national banks of the member states would be established. Reflecting a recognition of more modest aims for the CAU, it was also decided that the name of the organisation will be changed to the Central Asian Economic Community.

The Economic Cooperation Organisation (ECO)

The ECO was established in 1985 as the successor organisation to the Regional Cooperation for Development (RCD) formed in 1964. The RCD was established between Iran, Pakistan and Turkey but was largely inactive until relaunched in 1985. Soon after independence, the Central Asian states were quick to join the ECO. In its new guise, the ECO brings together ten member states with a potential market of over 325 million people. The ECO has emerged as an important forum for discussing common regional issues, but lacks the ability to become a more influential organisation.

As with the other interstate organisations of which Uzbekistan has become a member, co-operation within the ECO has been hampered by political competition between the founding members of the organisation. The diverse political objectives in the ECO have led to the emergence of subtle rivalries within the organisation. Initially, tension rivalry was focused on competition between Turkey and Iran for leadership of the organisation. Iran sought to stress its Islamic credentials for leading the ECO, while Turkey promoted itself as the secular model for the ECO's members. Pakistan too sought to position itself as a political force in the region through the ECO.

President Karimov has been highly suspicious of political aspirations articulated through the ECO and has viewed the organisation as a purely economic institution. In his July 1993 speech at a gathering of the ECO heads of state in Istanbul, Karimov addressed the issue of ideology:

> The first very important condition for us is the question of mutual trust. Naturally, the 10 members of the organization could have different views on policy and ideology ... unless we put economic interests higher than policy and ideology, there is no point to us meeting here, holding sessions, and going to all of this trouble.[18]

Uzbekistan has also been reluctant to enter into economic agreements with Iran for fear of importing or encouraging Islamic fundamentalism.

Despite Uzbekistan's resistance to turning the ECO into a political force, the organization has nevertheless achieved notable successes. In particular, the importance of the organisation for Uzbekistan has been focused on the construction of regional transport and communications infrastructure. One of the most significant ECO projects has been the agreement between Uzbekistan, Turkmenistan, Azerbaijan and Georgia to create a 'trans-Caspian transport corridor' extending from Tashkent to the port of Poti in Georgia. The corridor effectively established an export route for Uzbek goods beyond its traditional dependence on Russia and the Baltic ports. At the May 1998 ECO summit in Almaty, the focus was again on ways to improve transport and other communications between member states. The possibility of unifying customs tariffs and visa rules was also discussed. In 1998 it was decided to create the ECO Bank for Trade Development.

CONCLUSION

Since independence Tashkent has developed a complex web of foreign relations. Uzbekistan's external ties have been characterised by frequent reorientations reflecting the contradictory interests that have informed Uzbekistani foreign policy. Critical to the construction of Uzbekistan's international relations has been the form of domestic political and economic development that has emerged in the country.

In the early years of independence, the central factor driving the external relations of Uzbekistan was the imperative of promoting economic development in the country. The drive for financial assistance and the economic resources to modernise Uzbekistan led Tashkent to give priority to the development of relations with the advanced industrial powers and the allies of these states. Alongside economic growth, the aim of establishing an independent, Uzbekistan free from the legacy of the colonial (Russian) past, strongly informed Tashkent's approach to the external world. Finally, fostering relations with states and organisations that could strengthen the image of Uzbekistan as a secular nation-state was a priority.

Although the domestic agenda of economic modernisation initially provided the main impetus behind Tashkent's external agenda, relations with the outside world have since been heavily qualified by a number of other factors. The principal influences that have moderated the agenda of economic development established at independence have been President Karimov's efforts to ensure maintenance of the political regime that he has built since the late 1980s, and geopolitical and security concerns.

The authoritarian political regime developed under Karimov's tutelage initially undermined efforts to build good relations with the western powers. Tashkent was, however, gradually able to position itself as a security partner for the United States in the face of an apparent Islamic threat, a threat that was also linked to concerns about the future of the hydrocarbon resources of Central Asia (and western investment to develop these resources). Since 1995, Uzbekistan has emerged as the key element in western security and political policy towards Central Asia. The country, however, lags behind Kazakhstan in terms of economic relations with the West, although the pseudo-election of President Nazarbayev in 1999 may have soured Kazakhstan's political relationship with the West.

The landlocked status of Uzbekistan has also seen the return of geopolitics as an important factor in Central Asia, and a factor that has played a growing role in Uzbekistan's foreign policy. While relations with advanced industrial powers provided the primary focus of Uzbekistan's external relations, the growth of a variety of regional issues has required Tashkent to develop a diversity of relationships and alliances. Security issues resulting from the civil wars in Tajikistan and the Afghanistan, and the rise of political Islam in these areas has provided the catalyst for a moderation of the initial thrust to foreign policy.

While Tashkent's long-term aim may be to prevent Russia dominating the region, the immediate priorities of stemming the advance of political and military movements inspired by Islam has led Uzbekistan to court Moscow once again. The range of transborder issues within and around Central Asia have also required Uzbekistan to participate in a variety of interstate organisations, although the President appears to lack enthusiasm for such institutions. Karimov has continued to stress that Uzbekistan is following its own independent form of development.[19]

In many ways, external relations can be viewed as the most successful sphere of policy developed by President Karimov since independence. Uzbekistan has been able to pursue its main aim of building links to western industrial countries, particularly the United States, while still maintaining the wide variety of relations necessary to manage critical regional issues. All of this has been achieved with only minor threat to the domestic political regime, in the form of difficult relations with international financial organisations.

In recent years, Tashkent's apparent success in the external world has, however, been challenged by the clear failure of Karimov's policies towards Tajikistan and Afghanistan. The exclusion of representatives from the Uzbek minority in the peace process in Tajikistan and the inclusion of Islamic parties has forced a rapid revision of Tashkent's approach to the Tajik conflict. At the same time, the collapse of General Dostum's forces, Uzbekistan's ally, has left Karimov's policy towards Afghanistan in tatters.

The rapid fluctuations in the fortunes of Uzbekistani external policy suggest that Tashkent is likely to continue to struggle to remain ahead of developments in the region. Although the western powers have been partially engaged with the region, and Uzbekistan in particular, the relationship remains limited and fragile. A critical factor in the future of the region will be the role of Russia. If Moscow is unwilling or unable to maintain its current level of military and economic engagement with Central Asia, other external powers may be tempted to adopt a more assertive role towards the region. In this situation, Uzbekistan will most likely play a critical role in determining the future of Central Asia and its relations to the outside world.

1 *RFE/RL Newsline*, vol. 2, no. 121, part 1 (25 June 1998).
2 *RFE/RL Newsline*, vol. 2, no. 197, part 1 (12 October 1998).
3 *RFE/RL Newsline*, vol. 3, no. 25, part 1 (5 February 1999).
4 *RFE/RL Newsline*, vol. 2, no. 210, part 1 (30 October 1998).
5 *RFE/RL Newsline*, vol. 2, no. 90, part 1 (13 May 1998).
6 *RFE/RL Newsline*, vol. 2, no. 127, part 1 (3 July 1998).
7 Bohr, *op. cit.* (1998), p. 64.
8 *RFE/RL Newsline*, vol. 2, no. 211, part 1 (2 November 1998).
9 *RFE/RL Newsline*, vol. 3, no. 25, part 1 (5 February 1999).
10 *RFE/RL Newsline*, vol. 2, no. 211, part 1 (2 November 1998).
11 Quoted in Mehrdad Haghayeghi, 'Economic Cooperation Organization: A Preliminary Assessment', *Central Asian Monitor*, no. 1 (1995), p. 18.
12 *RFE/RL Newsline*, vol. 1, no. 157, part 1 (11 November 1997).

13 *RFE/RL Newsline*, vol. 2, no. 127, part 1 (3 July 1998).
14 Bohr, *op. cit.* (1998), p. 64.
15 *RFE/RL Newsline*, vol. 2, no. 211, part 1 (2 November 1998).
16 *RFE/RL Newsline*, vol. 3, no. 25, part 1 (5 February 1999).
17 *RFE/RL Newsline*, vol. 2, no. 211, part 1 (2 November 1998).
18 Quoted in Mehrdad Haghayeghi, 'Economic Cooperation Organization: A Preliminary Assessment', *Central Asian Monitor*, no. 1 (1995), p. 18.
19 *RFE/RL Newsline*, vol. 1, no. 157, part 1 (11 November 1997).

Conclusion

The establishment of Uzbekistan as an independent state at the end of 1991 marked a fundamental change in the political life of Central Asia. Although the Uzbek Soviet Socialist Republic had been fashioned as an administrative and cultural unit during the Soviet era, the demise of the Soviet state led to a basic shift in the nature and direction of the country's development and of Uzbekistan's significance for the rest of world. Since independence, Uzbekistan has become a leading element of Central Asia's regional political order, while beneath the veneer of stability and continuity there have been critical changes in the domestic order of the country.

Uzbekistan has been able to negotiate the first years of the post-Soviet order with a degree of success, or at least it has managed to avoid some of the disasters that have befallen other transitional societies (for example state collapse in Tajikistan, Georgia and Chechnia). Moreover, the new order that has been created under the leadership of President Karimov appears to enjoy widespread popular endorsement. Karimov continues to have high levels of personal support, although low expectations and a politically passive population make judging the actual level of backing for the regime problematic.

Despite the apparent ability of the system to deliver the political and economic environment that many in Uzbekistan feel is best suited to the country's circumstances, the appropriateness of the model of 'stability' and 'gradual' change that has been fostered needs careful evaluation. Uzbekistan has avoided the scenario of state collapse, but there has been a high price to pay for the type of regime that has been created.

Individual and collective freedoms have been trampled upon, the use of coercion and terror is widespread and the authorities have acted in an increasingly indiscriminate fashion in suppressing not simply opposition voices but all sources of independent opinion.[1] While the regime enjoys support from the populace for many of these policies, endorsement has often been manufactured by the authorities on the basis of the construction of futures that appear far worse (e.g. an Islamic state). Little effort has been given to exploring seriously alternative forms of development that incorporate genuine democratisation and economic liberalisation.

The key to Uzbekistan's post-independence programme of development is not, as official propaganda would have one believe, a careful and moderate process of change to maintain a delicate social and political balance in the country, but the radical and rapid reconfiguration of the country's political and economic order. In place of the Soviet-era authoritarian state, Uzbekistan has been transformed into a new type of authoritarian system based upon the unchecked power of the leader and the construction of a political economy to ensure the continuing functioning of this regime.

Within the system, broad-based political and economic development has been sacrificed to the interests of the Uzbekistani elite, particularly President Karimov. While the population continues to enjoy welfare benefits generally better that those available in other Central Asian states, this is not a viable long-term solution to the pressing need to create a successful, dynamic and efficient economy. Indeed, the distribution of welfare payments frequently appears more important as a means to stem popular discontent than for attacking the sources of poverty and inequality.

The emergence of the new order in Uzbekistan has numerous dimensions, but the construction of a new official ideology of Uzbek nationalism has been particularly important. Within this ideology the President and his drive to foster a highly centralised state based upon personalised rule is presented as the continuation of ancient traditions in the region. In Uzbekistan, President Karimov has frequently been compared to such notable figures as Timur. Indeed, the emergence of an Uzbekistani state with Karimov at its head often appears in official writings as the result of an organic and preordained process. In fact, the creation of this notion of historical evolution is the product of the exercise of state power to help forge a single national narrative from a fragmentary and contested past.[2]

While the establishment of a strong national identity is clearly an important element in the creation of a nation-state, the stress on the Uzbek elements of the past risks creating difficulties for the numerous minorities and cultures found in Uzbekistan. Moreover, the presence of large numbers of ethnic Uzbeks in neighbouring states suggests that significant tensions are likely to characterise interstate relations in the region as a result of competing loyalties and uncertain responsibilities.

A central part of the regime's strategy for Uzbekistan has been the stress on gradualist reform of the economy. Official figures suggest that Uzbekistan has experienced a far smaller economic decline than other post-Soviet states and that in some areas has even begun to achieve low levels of growth. Most independent observers are skeptical of government claims and point to a far less rosy future for the economy. In particular, external observers highlight the lack of structural reform and the continuing vulnerability of the economy to fluctuations in commodity prices for agricultural and minerals.

In fact, far from simply failing to reform the economy since independnce the regime in Uzbekistan has become ever more closely intertwined with business through state control and regulation, and the expansion of corruption. Political power has increasingly come to depend on the control of economic resources and the exercise of patrimonial authority. The close relationship of politics and business has been a key element in the spread of corruption in the country. Corruption has created serious problems for the operation of the national economy and in some areas may be beyond control. Breaking free from the dovetailing of political and economic power in Uzbekistan is going to be extremely difficult, even supposing there is a will amongst the elite to attempt this task.

International relations have been one of the few successes of the early years of independence, at least measured against the main aims for external relations established by President Karimov. Uzbekistan has been able to consolidate its position as a leading state in the Central Asia region and to develop a range of relationships to important states outside the region. Tashkent has managed to achieve considerable autonomy from Russia, although this also has much to do with Moscow's lack of a clear strategy for the Central Asian region and weakened international position. Tashkent has also been able to establish a working relationship with leading Western powers, notably the United States and the European Union, based upon the notion that Uzbekistan can serve as a strategic partner for the West in the region. The authoritarian nature of the regime in Uzbekistan, however, is likely to cause problems for this relationship in the future.

The increasing instability of the Central Asia region as whole, poses a significant challenge for Tashkent. Civil wars in Afghanistan and Tajikistan have frequently undermined Karimov's broader strategies in the region and threatened to have serious domestic implications for the Uzbekistani authorities. In recent years, fluctuations in regional relations have placed greater strains upon Uzbekistan's external policy causing a high degree of uncertainty about Tashkent's ability to manage it foreign relations.

Central to Uzbekistan's future will be its relationship to the international community. The country's complex geo-political situation, combined with the chronic economic problems faced by Tashkent has made building ties to the outside world extremely important. While Uzbekistan has been resistant to the type of economic reforms supported by international financial organisations, some efforts have been made to attract foreign investors and to diversify the economy. The country's generally difficult economic climate, however, has discouraged extensive engagement by outside investors, and foreign involvement remains limited to a few largely symbolic and high profile projects.

Equally important has been the political relationship to the international community. Although initially reluctant to develop close ties to Tashkent in the early years of independence, in recent years many leading powers have established far warmer relations with Uzbekistan, particularly in the sphere of military partnerships. The relationship to countries in North America and Western Europe remains, however, complex and riven with contradictions.

In this environment, the dilemma for developed nations regarding Uzbekistan is similar to that with other dictatorial countries. Many representatives of the business community believe that there are good opportunities for investment in Uzbekistan, although the rewards are only likely in the long-term. The democratic and human rights communities, on the other hand, have serious concerns about civil and political liberties and the country's ability to achieve a stable form of political development.

The central question for the international community and for the population in Uzbekistan is the durability of the system, particularly if the current presidential incumbent is removed from the scene. In Uzbekistan, the form of rule that has developed since independence means that the role of Karimov has become central to future development. The drive to consolidate power in the hands of the President has been achieved in the short-term, but long-term stability looks increasingly fragile.

Ironically, the measures that the President has employed to maintain his personal position above all others may be precisely what are promoting instability within and around the country. Critically, the actions of the existing regime have served to promote radical Islam as the only possible opposition to the policies of the government. More moderate voices of opposition or caution have been extinguished opening the way for a polarisation of society. With Karimov at the helm, the Uzbekistani state may be able to maintain the coherence to suppress opposition through crude methods of coercion and terror. If Karimov is removed, the regime lacks obvious and peaceful methods to produce a replacement. The President also takes great pains to ensure that no rivals for his position emerge from within the government. Without a genuine process of liberalisation to establish a more responsive political and economic system, the choice that faces Uzbekistan may increasingly become authoritarianism or anarchy.[3]

1 U.S. Department of State: Uzbekistan Country Report on Human Rights Practices for 1998 (http://www.state.gov/www/global/human_rights/1998_hrp_report/uzbekist.html).

2 Annette Bohr, 'The Central Asian States as nationalising regimes', in Graham Smith, Vivien Law, Andrew Wilson, Annette Bohr, Edward Allworth, *Nation-building in the Post-Soviet Borderlands: The Politics of National Identities* (Cambridge: CUP, 1998), pp. 139–64.

3 Anna Matveeva, 'Democratization, legitimacy and political change in Central Asia', *International Affairs*, vol. 75, number 1 (January 1999), pp. 36–7.

Bibliography

Edward Allworth, *Central Asia: 130 Years of Russian Dominance, A Historical Overview* (Durham: Duke University Press, 1994).

Edward A. Allworth, *The Modern Uzbeks: from the fourteenth century to the present: a cultural history* (Stanford, California: Hoover Press Publication, 1990).

John Anderson, *The International Politics of Central Asia* (Manchester: Manchester University Press, 1997).

Annette Bohr, *Uzbekistan: Politics and Foreign Policy* (London: Royal Institute of International Affairs, 1998).

William Fierman, 'Political Development in Uzbekistan: Democratization?', in Karen Dawisha and Bruce Parrott, eds., *Conflict, Cleavage and Change in Central Asia and the Caucasus* (Cambridge: Cambridge University Press, 1997), pp. 360–408.

http: freedomhouse.org/nil-98/uzbek.pdf.

Gregory Gleason, *The Central Asian States: Discovering Independence* (Boulder, Col.: Westview Press, 1997).

Henry Hale, 'Islam, State-building and Uzbekistan Foreign Policy', in Ali Banuazizi and Myron Weiner, eds., *The New Geopolitics of Central Asia and its Borderlands* (Bloomington, Indiana: Indiana University Press, 1994), pp. 136–72.

Mehrdad Haghayeghi, *Islam and Politics in Central Asia* (N.Y., N.Y.: St. Martin's Press, 1995).

Islam Karimov, *Uzbekistan on the Threshold of the Twenty-first Century* (Richmond, Surrey: Curzon Press, 1997).

Nancy Lubin, *Labour and Nationality in Soviet Central Asia: An Uneasy Compromise* (Princeton, NJ: Princeton University Press).

Michael Rywkin, *Moscow's Muslim Challenge: Soviet Central Asia* (London: M. E. Sharpe, 1990).

U.S. Department of State, *Uzbekistan Country Report on Human Rights Practices for 1998* (http://www.state.gov/www/global/human_rights/1998_hrp_report/uzbekist.html).

Index

For Product Safety Concerns and Information please contact our EU
representative GPSR@taylorandfrancis.com
Taylor & Francis Verlag GmbH, Kaufingerstraße 24, 80331 München, Germany

www.ingramcontent.com/pod-product-compliance
Ingram Content Group UK Ltd.
Pitfield, Milton Keynes, MK11 3LW, UK
UKHW022122190926
475702UK00013B/1597
9789058230300